John Walters sat ... holidays had been ... -seen animal pushi... through the bracken. But why di... movement stop so suddenly?

That was the start of the terrific adventure which finished the holidays in a blaze of excitement. For the animal had disappeared into an undiscovered cave, which stretched far away into the hill, and John and his friends could not rest until they had explored the cave's tantalizing mysteries.

But it is what happens to them *inside* the cave that makes this book especially good, for the characters of the five friends change and develop in face of the dangers they encounter.

Richard Church is a fine writer for adults and brings just as much skill and perception into this story for readers of nine and over.

Cover design by David Knight

RICHARD CHURCH

THE CAVE

'We have come under this
cavern's roof'
THE GREEK EMPEDOCLES

Illustrated by Geoffrey Whittam

PENGUIN BOOKS

Penguin Books Ltd, Harmondsworth, Middlesex, England
Penguin Books Australia Ltd, Ringwood, Victoria, Australia

—

First published by Dent 1950
Revised edition published by William Heinemann Ltd 1960
Published in Puffin Books 1966
Reprinted 1968, 1970

—

—

Made and printed in Great Britain
by Richard Clay (The Chaucer Press), Ltd,
Bungay, Suffolk
Set in Linotype Granjon

CONTENTS

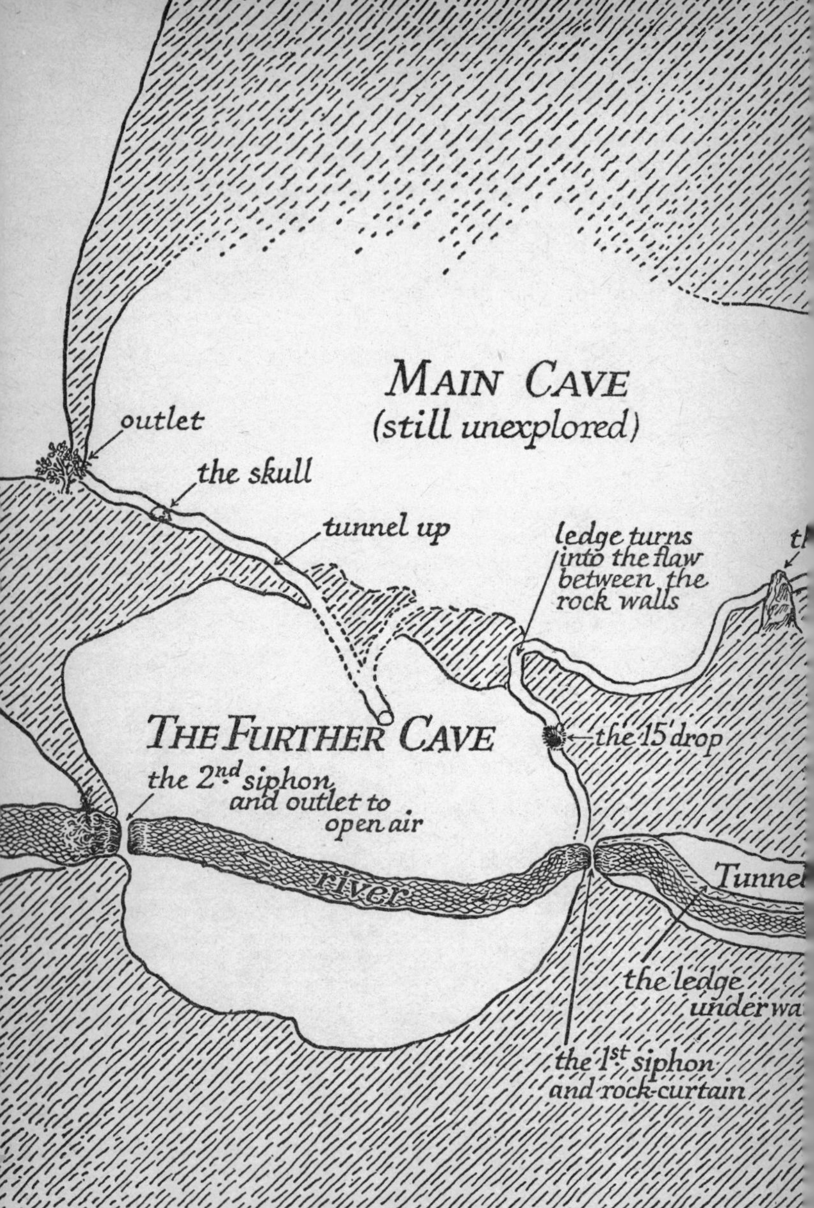
MAIN CAVE
(still unexplored)
outlet
the skull
tunnel up
ledge turns into the flaw between the rock walls
THE FURTHER CAVE
the 15' drop
the 2nd. siphon and outlet to open air
river
the ledge
the 1st. siphon and rock-curtain
R·L·K·

The shaded areas indicate solid rock

CHAPTER I

A SEA OF BRACKEN

JOHN WALTERS sat on a rock sticking up out of a sea of bracken. He was thinking about the summer holidays. A month ago they had still stretched in front of him without an end in sight; but now only two weeks remained, and he felt as though nothing had been done and too many summer days wasted in pottering about. There were reasons for that. All families have their troubles, and he knew that his parents had been having a rough passage although they told him little about it. He thought of them now, and of the wonderful time which had been promised him and his younger brother; a boating expedition on the Broads. All that had come to nothing and here he had been more or less alone in the country home of his uncle and aunt, Dr George and Mary Walters, while his young brother had been sent off to other relations.

He sat on the top of the rock like Napoleon on St Helena, lonely and bored. The afternoon sun of an early September day was sinking westward. He felt it burning his back as he stared, without seeing, along the vast stretch of four-foot-high bracken which lay between him and the out-cropping of other rocks at the foot of the limestone hills. Those hills now blazed in the heat and light of the sun. The sky above them was pale blue with feathery wisps of motion-less cloud. The only sound to be heard was the steady drone of myriads of insects' wings. A salty smell, like that of the sea, rose from the bracken. John saw, heard and smelled, but he registered nothing. He was really miserable and he could not understand why. He tried to imagine what it might be that made him so doleful, and suddenly he realized that it was six o'clock on a Sunday evening, that time of week when the bottom seems to drop out of life and nothing is real. In order to cheer himself up he took off his new spectacles and examined them with pleasure. They had gold rims, and he was proud of them; doubly proud because when he had been told that he would have to wear spectacles to correct short sight he had been furious with rage, believing that this would disqualify him from all the things that were worth while; cricket, swimming, climbing and all the other active pursuits of life. He had found his fears to be groundless, however, and the exciting view which the spectacles had brought to him of things hitherto vague and misty, had filled his days with an added keenness, if that were possible.

As he wiped his lenses on a little piece of wash-leather, which his father had given him, he heard a faint disturbance. It proved to be the distant cawing of a flight of rooks, winging their way in loose formation towards the sunset. He quickly put on his spectacles and saw the birds coming over him, high up. Each one was distinct and he could see its wing feathers as the great pinions moved in rhythm with the raucous voices.

With his attention fixed on this splendid sight, he forgot his gloomy thoughts and remained face upwards to the sky while the birds drew near, passed overhead and dwindled towards the west. In order to watch the last of them he lay back on the rock and stared into the sky from this topsy-turvy position, so that when he sat up again, a film of reddish colour floated for an instant between him and the familiar view of the bracken, the rocks and the distant hills. When the film cleared he felt his clarity of vision even sharper than before. It was so sharp, indeed, that he began consciously to test it by singling out first near-by fronds of the fern and then more and more distant ones, until he could trace almost microscopic details of leaf formation on the distant edge where the sea of bracken seemed to break in green foam against those massive rocks of which the one where he sat was an odd outrider.

Then his attention was switched to a more immediate matter. Slowly, across his line of vision, a wave disturbed the bracken, like the wake of a ship in the sea. Something was moving eastward towards the rocks. The whole of the landscape was dead still except for this movement. The rooks had disappeared, and the clouds hung motionless. He watched the swaying fronds as they parted and closed again over the disturbance from the creature active beneath them.

Parting the bracken with both arms he peered down

It was a sight to rouse the most idle person's curiosity. And John Walters was anything but an idle person. He was a great enjoyer of life in his quiet way; a person who liked to get things going, and to make friends in the process.

So there he sat with body and mind tense, concentrating on this interesting spectacle, the first sign of life observed during the whole of an idle Sunday afternoon towards the end of an uneventful holiday. The movement in the green bracken continued without swerving to right or to left. Whatever the creature was, it knew definitely where it wanted to go, like a submarine making for its prey. At one moment the movement stopped and the bracken swung back into silence and stillness. John fixed his gaze on the point where the wave had ceased, and he was preparing to scramble down the rock and to make his way there when the wave began again and proceeded without further interruption as straight as an arrow-shot until it reached the smaller of two rocks that leaned towards each other like fragments of a Stone-Age worshipping place. The bracken surged up against them as though it intended to devour a mountain-ash tree which grew in front of them, half of it in the sun with gleaming red berries, the other half in the shadow of the rocks. The movement in the bracken reached the tree and then broke into confusion where the creature was beating about before finding what it wanted.

John left his observation post, and, in leaping to the ground, twisted his ankle. He was so excited, however, that he ignored the sharp pain and limped on, pushing the bracken aside with the stout ash stick which he had cut at the beginning of the holidays and decorated with his initials and the symbol of an axe-head. A particularly obstinate bracken stalk tripped him up, but the foliage was so thick that he felt the fall as though it were on to a spring mattress. He was up again in an instant; the pain in his ankle vanished.

At last he reached the rowan tree. There was nothing to be seen. Not a movement, not a sound betrayed anything to the inquisitive boy. He was nonplussed, and stood for some moments prodding about with his stick, at a loss what to do next. Then suddenly, as he poked the stick through the bracken under the shelter of the smaller rock in the shadow of the tree, he felt it go through into space instead of touching firm ground. He prodded about further and felt an edge which suggested that he had struck a hole. Parting the bracken with both arms he peered down and saw before him a hollow caused by decay at ground level in the surface of the rock, and through this fracture a cavernous opening about four feet in diameter. It was obviously an ancient rift because it was covered by various coloured mosses and festooned with little harts' tongue ferns, some of which were crimson and liver coloured. Just inside the mouth of the opening stood a cluster of flesh-tinted fungi, many of them broken off. He felt a waft of coldish air scented with water and a sepulchral odour which he could not recognize. It was frightening; it was exciting.

Excitement won, and after probing with his stick, he crawled into the hole head first and found himself in a narrow tunnel that sloped down gently for several yards, then more sharply. Inch by inch, he felt his way down into the darkness. He could feel his heart thumping in his chest which was pressed to the ground. He crawled on for two or three feet and felt the moss give place to bare rock which was cold and damp. Then fear overcame curiosity and he stopped crawling. Silence fell about him, the uncanny silence which is found only in confined spaces. He tried to look ahead but could see nothing. He turned first one ear and then the other towards the unknown and for one second he thought he heard a faint murmur, it might be of departing footsteps, or a distant trickle of water.

By now, his eyes had grown accustomed to the darkness. By pressing his body towards one wall of the tunnel he allowed a little light to pass him and reveal an alteration in the rock form some six feet ahead. It was safe, at any rate, to crawl as far as that. This he did, and putting forward one arm with the stick held out in front of him, and tapping gently downwards, he became aware that the passage ended abruptly, dropping into a space that offered infinite possibilities of adventure and unknown peril.

CHAPTER 2

FOOD FOR THOUGHT

It was not until this moment that he realized he was alone. The excitement of the adventure had seemed to supply him with an imaginary companion with whom he could exchange confidences, and from whom he could seek advice. But now he knew that this was but a trick of his imagination, and that the whole responsibility of the next step remained with himself. What was that step to be? If he went on alone and got into difficulties the results might be horrible, for probably no human being knew of this hole in the earth. It had obviously not been disturbed for many summers, as the mossy growth around the entrance indicated. If he went back now, however, would that mean that he was afraid?

He decided that it was unnecessary to answer this last question. Only a fool would run into unnecessary danger without preparation. That was the point; preparations must be made for the next step, just as in a war, or a polar expedition.

While he was thinking these things out he lay flat on his stomach with his head projecting over the edge above the unknown depth. He could now hear the faint drip of water and farther off to the left a tiny trickling sound, which suggested a running stream and a chamber of considerable size. He tried to turn his head to look upwards for a roof, but this effort caused him to move his shoulders and thus dislodge some fragments of loose soil from the top of the tunnel above him, which filled his hair and his right ear. 'Lucky it wasn't my eye,' he said to himself. To his surprise, he found that he had spoken aloud, and he heard a semi-echo of his own voice come back at him from what must have been the farther wall of the nothingness before him. It was awe-inspiring, and he was reminded still more forcibly that he was alone on the threshold of an underworld in the depths of the earth.

He now determined to return on his tracks and to think things out. Wriggling backwards, however, was a different matter from crawling forward. For one thing his coat, which had been done up by the bottom button over his pull-over, was now dragged upwards under his armpits to form a thick pad that stopped his movements. He had to leave go of his stick and struggle to drag his coat down, and this effort pulled the button off. He turned on his side, did up the other two buttons, slipped off his belt and put it on outside his coat. He was thus able to make his way backwards up the passage until he came to the mossy entrance.

He felt as though he were stepping out into the heat of an oven. He looked at his hands and saw that they were blue with cold. The excitement and the change of temperature after the struggle in an unaccustomed position made him break into a hearty sweat. He found, too, a smear of greasy clay down the front of his trousers and coat. He would have some explaining to do when he reached his aunt's house, but she was a tolerant person, and he was not much worried. Before going back to supper, he wanted to think out what the next approach to the cave would be. There was no question of not returning, for this was indeed an adventure to make a holiday worth while. His gloomy thoughts about missed opportunities on the Norfolk Broads were already forgotten.

Picking a bunch of red berries off the rowan tree, he sat down with them in his hand and used them, berry by berry, as counters to mark the items as he went over in his mind what equipment would be necessary for exploring the cave. He laid the berries, one by one, in a square formation on a little ledge of rock where he had been sitting, facing the sun, which now blazed across the river that ran below the moorland a mile west of the rocks and the rising foothills before turning north to the estuary.

John decided that first he would need a rope. But a rope would be useless without a companion, and this led him to another problem. During the holidays he had been initiated, by the boy living in the house next door to his uncle's, into a secret society consisting of four schoolfellows, three of whom had failed to get away from their native town for a holiday that summer. As the town was new to John, and situated between hills and sea, he did not think this hardship sat very heavily on the shoulders of his holiday confederates. They certainly seemed a cheerful set and had been very decent to him, a stranger. He realized now that he owed it to them to introduce them to this adventure, and, therefore, the next thing to do was to summon a council as speedily as possible. That being so, he would need to be ready with his suggestions, and the more practical they were, the better reception they would have. So he repeated to himself: item, one stout rope. Then he considered that there would probably be further tunnels to be negotiated, and these might give occasion when it would be necessary to knock away pieces of rock before progress could be made. For this sort of job, a hammer and cold chisel would be needed, and a small spade or trenching tool to remove the chips. Most important of all, he would need torches, several electric torches, in case one should give out or be broken.

Having thought things out so far, John had mastered the first excitement of his discovery, and he made his way back to the outskirts of the town. By that time the damp clay on his clothes had dried off somewhat, enabling him to brush down and generally tidy up before entering the house.

He was about to turn in at the gate of the short drive to his uncle's house when he heard a long whistle from the farther gate beyond a small copse. It was a call from his temporary neighbour, George Reynolds, the boy who had introduced him to the Tomahawk Club, whose sign was the axe-head which John had carved on his ash stick.

Without waiting for the other boy to approach he ran on and confronted George with a breathless, muddied oaf whose bespectacled eyes shone in the gathering dusk with a feverish intensity.

'What's up?' asked George, who spoke with a curiously

'I *have* found something! We must get the Tomahawks together!'

husky voice. 'You look as though you have found something.'

'I have,' John almost shouted, 'I *have* found something! We must get the Tomahawks together!' Then controlling himself as far as he was able, he told George about his discovery, with the result that his friend undertook to call the members to a meeting in the boat-house by the river at the bottom of his garden. He told John to be confident of a full attendance at nine o'clock next morning. With that they separated, and John went in to his supper and the kindly company of his childless uncle and aunt.

The latter met him in the hall and looked him up and down.

'I'm glad I don't have to buy your suits,' she said trying to be severe. 'Whatever have you been up to?'

John examined his ravaged clothes, with a pretence of surprise.

'We've just been crawling about a bit,' he said, and this reply, delivered with such a stupid air, so amused his aunt that she laughed, and ruffled his already tousled hair.

'You ragamuffin!' she said, still chuckling. 'And you've torn a button off your coat. I doubt if I have one to match. You'll have to go in rags until you find that lost button.'

CHAPTER 3

A COUNCIL OF ACTION

JOHN woke up in the night and looked at his new wristwatch to find that the time was half past two. After enjoying the fact that he could read the time in the dark because his watch had luminous hands, he realized that he had awakened as a result of the excitement that filled his mind. Lying in the darkness he imagined that he was already on an expedition in the midst of a series of underground vaults of colossal dimensions; but being a practical boy he soon turned from this vague speculation to a concern about ways and means. Over and over in his mind went that list of things which would be needed in the exploration of whatever lay beyond that short natural chimney into which he had ventured last evening. The effort of counting the items one by one lulled him to sleep again, and the next thing he realized was that his uncle was standing over him with a cup of tea, and stirring it with a spoon that caught the sunlight and flashed wild messages round the walls and ceiling.

'You must have been dreaming,' said his uncle, lighting another cigarette. 'Your bed looks like an earthquake. I have just been called out to a patient, so bang goes my breakfast. A doctor's life is a dog's life.' His broad face with its grin of good humour and understanding, however, much belied his words. 'Would you like a car ride?' he added.

John sat up abruptly.

'Rather,' he murmured, still half asleep. Then he remembered. 'No thanks, uncle,' he said with some confusion, 'I've got a meeting this morning.'

This remark appeared to amuse his uncle as much as his words last night had amused his aunt.

'You're an old-fashioned party,' said the doctor, 'and a

quiet one, too.' And with that he departed, leaving John to swallow the tea and scramble down to breakfast.

Nine o'clock found him slipping through the gate into the copse at the bottom of the garden where a path led down to the river. He whistled as he went and a reply through the trees told him that at least one member of the Tomahawk Club had arrived. It proved to be a boy named Harold Soames, a tiny little chap who was always in front of time and in a desperate hurry. He was an only boy among an army of older sisters, and for lack of opportunity had got into the habit of seldom speaking. He always acted first, and this made him a reckless character. He was good looking, and hated his good looks.

This morning, however, he was the first to speak, and what he said was in keeping with his reputation. 'Shall we go now?' he cried, in a voice like a bosun's whistle.

John looked at him through those calm spectacles and this appeared to sober him down.

'Go where?' said John.

Before Soames could find words to reply, other members began to arrive. George Reynolds approached with a fat boy named Cuthbert Sanders, who because of his bulk was known as Meaty. He was so stout that George by comparison rattled like a skeleton, especially when he gave vent to that husky voice for which he was famous.

They entered the boat-house and sat waiting for the fifth member, Alan Hobbs, a boy who was always late. The open end of the building faced east on to the water and thus the morning sun was reflected into the semi-darkness. Swords of light flashed across the ceiling, and graceful shapes leaped about the walls in rhythm with the wavelets on the river. John was reminded of the spoon with his early cup of tea. There was only one boat in the shed, half sunk in the watery inlet which was part of the floor of the place. The usual junk filled every other corner; pots of paint, brooms and brushes, broken fishing rods, boat hooks and oars, coils of rope and a carpenter's bench in a disgraceful state of neglect with its tools rusted. A dark-lantern stood on the bench, draped in cobwebs. The whole scene looked like a picture painted a hundred years ago. The Tomahawk Club was not worried by this, nor by the lateness of its missing member. In response to three eager inquiries, John began to tell of his discovery. Before he had got far into the narrative, Alan Hobbs arrived. The newcomer immediately stopped the proceedings. How he did so nobody knew. It must have been the way he was made. He was tall, upright, with fair hair thrown right back. He had a strong, dominating voice that overrode any opposition. Usually none was offered. He now took the lead on the assumption that nothing could possibly have been started before he arrived.

'What's this, George?' he asked, ignoring the fact that it was John who had made the occasion for this summary meeting of the Tomahawk Club. George however, had no desire to shine, and he turned to John who quietly began his story for the second time; more quietly, indeed, now that Alan Hobbs was present.

The effect on Alan was spectacular. At first he listened with amused tolerance; but as his imagination caught fire he grew more and more restless until at last he could contain himself no longer.

'But this is tremendous,' he burst out, interrupting John. 'You don't realize, you fellows, you don't realize what the possibilities are. I know all about exploring caves. My father says it's the foundation of our knowledge of the human race. Men lived in caves during the Ice Age, and it's quite likely we shall find relics of them. Sometimes there are paintings on the walls, hunting scenes, and all that. We shall find weapons, too, and be able to send them to the British Museum. It'll be tremendous!'

He was already excited by the prospect of such fame, and his face had lost its rather peevish look and shone like that of a hero, as the little splashes of light illuminated it under the chin, nostrils and eyebrows. All the boys were impressed, and there was a moment's silence while he gathered himself up to say something even more impressive, but as he was about to speak, Meaty Sanders spoiled the occasion by murmuring: 'We'd better take sandwiches with us, for it might be a long job.' This provoked laughter and brought the project down to earth, with the result that a discussion followed as to ways and means of supplying the necessary equipment, during which Alan alternated between his habitual aloofness and sudden entries into the argument when a point stirred his ever-ready sense of the dramatic. It was obvious that he was impatient with the cool manner in which John enumerated the list of things required, and it might even be that he resented the attention being given to the originator of the adventure.

'We shall need several coils of rope and, better still, a rope ladder,' said John, in his solemn way. 'Perhaps we can find enough here,' and he nodded at three respective corners of the dusky boat-house. 'We shall also want a hammer and cold chisel and a shovel; yes, and candles and matches as well as torches. Has everybody got a torch?'

This question stirred Alan Hobbs again.

'Yes,' he shouted. 'I'll borrow my father's electric lantern, it shows a straight beam and has a strong bull's eye, as well. It's no use your taking that old thing,' he added, turning to George and pointing to the dark-lantern on the bench. 'It would only overheat and smoke in a confined space.'

'We might cook bloaters over it,' said Meaty, who was sometimes suspected of being a humorist.

Nobody had suggested taking the old-fashioned lantern, but that didn't matter. Alan Hobbs had found a chance to show his authority as self-appointed president of the Tomahawk Club. His speech so impressed the company that Meaty's remark about the bloaters was ignored and everybody sat silent for a few moments. George was the first to speak.

'I should say the all-important thing is our system of lighting. It would be fatal to be lost underground in complete darkness, and that means we must be ready for accidents. Each of us needs a hand torch or a bicycle lamp, and, if possible, a new spare battery and a bulb.' Then he added in his sepulchral voice, like the croak of a raven, 'Suppose we got cut off.'

This solemn remark made everybody realize the seriousness of the undertaking, and again there was a pause a minute or two while the members thought things over. At the end of it little Harold Soames suddenly plunged a hand into his trouser pocket and produced a compass, which he held out at arm's length.

'Look,' he said, 'I'd forgotten this; we can't go without a compass, for these underground passages wind about and we should lose our sense of direction.'

This was impressive, and Harold became the centre of interest, a situation which caused Alan to take immediate action.

'Is it a prismatic?' he asked, looking down at Harold. 'My uncle has promised me an Air Force one, and they're all prismatic. He flew in Mosquitoes during the war, and got the D.F.C. and Bar. My father says that only prismatic compasses are absolutely reliable.'

'Oh!' said Harold, rather flattened; but he cheered up immediately when John held out a hand to take the compass, saying: 'That's a brainwave of yours, Lightning. Many thanks.' Lightning was the name given to Harold by the club because that was the way he moved and thought and had his being.

He was so restored by this encouragement that he made another suggestion.

'I read in a book that it's a good idea to take a ball of twine to unroll as you go along so that you can find your way back.'

'What's the difference between twine and string?' asked

Meaty Sanders; but again his remark was ignored because nobody could be sure whether he was being humorous or was merely buried alive in his own flesh. But he never minded these snubs. 'I suppose twine costs more,' he concluded.

After these asides, John brought the discussion back by suggesting that everyone should bring a candle and a box of matches, enough food to last for a day and a bottle or scout's flask of water. 'Of course, everybody's got a pocket knife,' he added. A final suggestion was made by George, who gloomily remarked that each member should carry a small scribbling-pad and a pencil so that he could leave messages if he were cut off by some unforeseen disaster. Everybody took that seriously and agreed to do so.

After that, the party broke up on an outburst of enthusiasm and lust for action. It was John who quietly inquired who was to supply the rope, who the tools and who the food and so forth.

'Of course,' shouted Alan, 'let's be systematic, or we shall have too much of one thing.' And he began to give orders to each in turn in such an impressive way that nobody disagreed, although there must have been many doubts about the possibility of each member being able to provide the articles assigned to him by the leader. For it was assumed by now that Alan would be the leader of the exploration. 'I suggest,' he said finally, 'that we ought to start on Wednesday morning. That gives us two clear days to make our preparations and to get everything ready. You've got to remember that something big may come of this. I mean that we may find all sorts of treasure: hidden gold, extinct animals! Why, it's tremendous!' His face was alight again with an excitement that stirred the imagination of everybody present and made him readily acceptable as captain, although it was a position to which he had appointed himself without hesitation.

It was John who sorted things out, as it were in the background, and arranged about the provision of the things required, and fixed the assembly for nine o'clock on Wednesday morning. Everyone, except perhaps Alan, would have preferred to start at daybreak, but this would have involved taking people at home into their confidence, and that might have brought objections from certain timid parents. Harold Soames thought anxiously of his army of sisters, and he, for one, welcomed the present arrangement.

CHAPTER 4

PREPARING FOR THE ADVENTURE

THE members of the Tomahawk Club had two busy days. The problem of collecting the things they wanted was not an easy one because it had to be done on the understanding that there would be no opposition from the world of grown-ups. John Walters lingered on in the boat-house with his neighbour, George, after the other members had gone, and the two boys made a systematic examination of every loose object in the tumble-down building. First they examined the dark-lantern and decided that it was too much of an antique to be of any use. For one thing, it had no wick. In a corner under the carpenter's bench, John found a box containing a lot of cleaning rags, and underneath them a huge ball of tarred string. He held it up in his hand and turned to George who was standing thoughtfully contemplating the dark-lantern again.

'Look here,' he said, 'you remember what Lightning suggested? Here is the very thing, there must be hundreds of feet of it. We ought to find this useful.' He set it on the bench and continued his research beneath.

Half an hour later they had accumulated a large quantity of rope, sufficient to make a rope ladder, two cold chisels and hammers, a trenching tool and a comparatively unused picnic basket which contained a spirit lamp.

The boys then parted, and John now had the idea that a look round his uncle's garage would be profitable. The doctor had been a mountaineer and was still a member of the famous Alpine Club. There might be relics of his activities stowed away in the loft above the great garage which was an adapted barn. His search, however, was at first disappointing, for unlike the Reynolds' boat-house this place was kept spick and span, although his uncle, like most country practitioners, was a busy man. A large locked cupboard filled John with curiosity; but there was nothing to be done about it. He was clambering down from the loft when he heard the car drive in and his uncle caught him when he was half-way down the ladder.

'Hallo,' said the doctor, 'You've got through your meeting then? What happens next?'

John was suddenly inspired to a rash act. He had seen a gleam of subtle understanding in his uncle's eye. Before he could restrain himself he had poured out the tale about his discovery of the cave mouth and how the five boys were planning to explore farther.

'The trouble is,' he said solemnly, 'that some of the fellows' people may object. Harold Soames, for instance, he's got a lot of sisters who keep him wrapped in cotton wool, or try to.'

The perplexity on his face again seemed to amuse his uncle who said with an air of conspiracy, 'Yes, my boy, and you've got an aunt who feels heavily responsible while you are under her roof. You can't blame her for that, and as I'm married to her, I must back her up. But I think no fellow should miss a chance of exploring a cave or a mountain or anything that will test his muscles and his brain. So just you climb back into that loft, and we will see if we can find something to help the good work.'

John, who had been inclined to curse himself for an impetuous fool as soon as he had confided in his uncle, was now reassured, and he climbed the ladder to the loft eagerly. The doctor, looking thoughtful and profoundly serious, so serious indeed that John suspected him of acting a part, produced a bunch of keys from his pocket, selected one and unlocked the door of the cupboard.

'I'm now about to reveal my past,' he said, throwing back the double doors.

John saw a mountaineer's equipment.

'There you are,' said Dr Walters, 'take a look at that museum.' There was a note of wistfulness in his voice. 'You ought to find one or two things there that will come in handy.' He reached up and took down a neatly coiled rope which had been lovingly preserved. 'Be careful how you handle that. See that there are no chafing edges for it to rub against, especially if you've got a man hanging on the end and his life depends on it. There's one thing to remember when people are not sure of their footing on a dangerous spot, and that is the mountaineer's clasp.'

He showed John how two people grip each other round the wrist, thus making a doubly strong human joint. He then inquired about the boys' plans for lighting, and nodded his head in approval when John said that each one of them had agreed to bring a torch with a spare battery and bulb.

'But you'll need candles, as well,' he said, 'because they're useful not only as an emergency light but as a test for bad air. Where a candle flame dies out you can look for trouble. You might as well be doubly armed in this matter of lighting and I'll lend you a little pocket torch which most doctors carry. It'll go into your pocket like a pen and you can forget all about it. You might get into a tight corner where it would come in useful.' Then he looked John straight in the eye in that quiet grave way which gave such confidence. 'The point is this, John; on jobs of this kind a man has to think of everything beforehand. This adventure is your idea, and that means that you are responsible for the safety of those other fellows as well as your own.' Then his face creased into a smile. 'That's all! I've finished my sermon. All I hope is that your aunt doesn't find out what's afoot before Wednesday morning. And the same applies to the womenfolk of the other chaps, whoever they are. I'd better not know their names!'

He turned towards the trap door of the loft and was descending, when he was arrested by a second thought. Popping his head up again above the level of the floor he said, 'Look here, John, I'm with you over this business because I am confident that you'll make a good job of it. I'll make this stipulation, that you must be back before dinner that night. If you are not here by seven o'clock I shall have to come and look for you and I shall be in a bad temper. I want you secretly to draw me a plan of the mouth of the cave, showing where it is. For that purpose you'd better pay it another visit this afternoon and calculate your distances as precisely as you can. Put that plan into an envelope and seal it up and leave it under the blotting pad on the desk in the surgery. When you get home safely, I will give it back to you unopened and the cave will still remain your secret. That's all I've got to say, except that you'll find a small first-aid kit in the pocket of your mackintosh hanging in the hall. Pick that up as you go out and be sure you don't forget it.'

Uncle and nephew entered the house together looking as unlike conspirators as they possibly could. John, perhaps over-anxious, sat at the table and took an occasional glance at his aunt. He wondered once or twice what was meant by her downcast eyes and the ghost of a demure smile which visited her face after she had given both him and her husband a shrewd womanly look. The doctor deliberately refrained from challenging this inquiry, and addressed himself innocently to his meal and a general conversation about the affairs of the day.

'John dear,' said his aunt at the end of the meal, 'would you care to invite your friend George, from next door, to dinner one evening?' She turned to her husband, 'That boy worries me, he's a walking skeleton, and I'm sure he is not properly fed in that chaotic household.'

'Now, now,' said the doctor. 'No gossip! Not a whisper! But it's a brave idea, my love. Ask him in tomorrow night, John, and we'll slaughter a hen in his honour.'

John fancied that he saw the beginning of a wink from

his uncle's right eye. But it was only a fancy, for the face of the doctor at once became a professional mask as he departed to his surgery for the hour's session before starting off on his afternoon round.

John thanked his aunt and said he would be delighted to invite George. He was not really delighted, however, for he felt that the less he and his confederates were in contact with parents and guardians during the next forty-eight hours, the better it would be for the security of the plans for the forthcoming campaign. But he knew that the poker-faced George was not an easy book to read, even by so acute a person as his Aunt Mary, who had once been a sister in a large London hospital, and knew something about human nature.

John wandered off to his own room and read for a quarter of an hour. Then thinking the coast was clear he put an envelope in his pocket and went out with a drawing-block and pencil. Leaving the outskirts of the town he cut across the fields, and within ten minutes had reached the familiar scrubland where the sea of bracken began its gradual slope towards the rocks and the hills at whose extreme edge, a mile to the west, the river made its magnificent sweep.

The scene was different from what it had been the night before. A stiff breeze was blowing up the river round the end of the hills, carrying with it a slight sea-mist, whose salt could be savoured on the lips. The bracken seemed to flow in a green tide as the wind passed over it, creating the semblance of wave after wave moving eastward and breaking on the rocks. The mist piled up, changing the sun to a silver medal and turning the air to a chilly fabric that could be touched like cobweb.

John followed a rabbit-run through the bracken to the rock where he had been lying the previous evening. His progress was slow because he was measuring his paces, reckoning each one at three feet. He noted down that the rock was two hundred yards from the field gate where he had entered the commonland. He turned round and looked up at the sun, and realized how badly he needed a compass. This reminded him of Harold Soames, and once more he was grateful to that lively little customer for the contribution of a compass towards Wednesday's expedition. He had now, however, to make do without the instrument. Looking at his watch, he saw that the hour was precisely four o'clock and he knew that, allowing for summer-time, this meant that the sun was due south-west. He also noted that it stood exactly over the field gate, and from this he was able to record on his drawing-block that the path to the cave ran first due north-east from the gate to the large rock standing isolated in the middle of the sea of bracken. He then looked in the opposite direction for the tree of mountain-ash with its red berries.

At that moment a gust of wind beat back from the hills and threw a scarf of mist in front of the rocks. John waited patiently, content to watch the curious and tortured folds of the mist which obscured his view. At the same time he recollected the movement in the bracken yesterday which had first drawn him to the entrance of the cave. If the same creature which had caused that movement were out today; it was certainly safe from observation, for now the bracken was dancing and heaving in all directions, like a cornfield in July. He found himself wondering what that animal might have been, and he was amused to find that he had not given the matter another thought since the excitement of the discovery of the cave. Whatever it was, he was grateful to the unknown animal, whether mastodon or mouse.

The scarf of mist had now blown away and there stood the rowan tree with its little berries burning like lamps in the moist air. Raising one arm in the direction of the sun, he lifted the other to point towards the tree and then began to calculate the angle made by his two arms. He thus estimated roughly that the tree lay due north from the rock in the middle of the bracken patch.

John next paced out the ground between himself and the rowan tree. This was no easy matter because it involved treading down the tough late-summer bracken which was whipping about like snakes between his legs. At last, however, he reached the foot of the tree after measuring some two hundred and fifty yards from the rocks. He was about to note this at the corner of the block on which he intended to make the map, when his attention was arrested by a scuffling noise from the dark shadow which the tree cast on the incurving side of the rock overhanging the entrance to the cave. Pausing for a moment to jot down the figures systematically, in case he forgot them, he trod three stealthy paces forward towards the entrance. That methodical pause, however, had given the creature time to disappear, either into the cavern or out beneath the concealing tumult of the bracken. John's curiosity had again to remain unsatisfied. He could not now grope into the cave because he knew that his aunt wanted him to get back in a reasonably tidy condition to meet some visitors for tea. He decided to sit on the little ledge and to draw his map. He turned round with this intention and there saw a spectacle which, for some moments, made him forget his purpose. A large grey squirrel was squatting on the ledge sampling, one by one, the berries which John had laid out the previous evening as counters when making up the list of things required for the expedition. The squirrel appeared not to appreciate the catalogue. He picked up one berry, examined it with a protruding and beady eye, scraped it with his incisive teeth and then threw it aside. There went the coil of rope, thought John. The next berry, representing the electric torches, followed suit, and so the process of rejection went on until the ledge was cleared. The incident was so comical that the boy laughed aloud. Instantly the squirrel leapt round, glared at John with indignation, shivered, then took a flying leap and landed in the boughs of the rowan tree. From there he leapt to the top of the rock and disappeared over it, no doubt making for a large oak tree which stood on the other side as a forerunner to a little clump of woodland.

At any other time John would have followed up so inviting a hunt, but today his mind was concentrated on one thing only, and that was the making of the map so that he could repay his uncle's trust. Dr Walters was that sort of man. So within a few moments of the disappearance of the squirrel, John was sitting once more on the ledge of rock

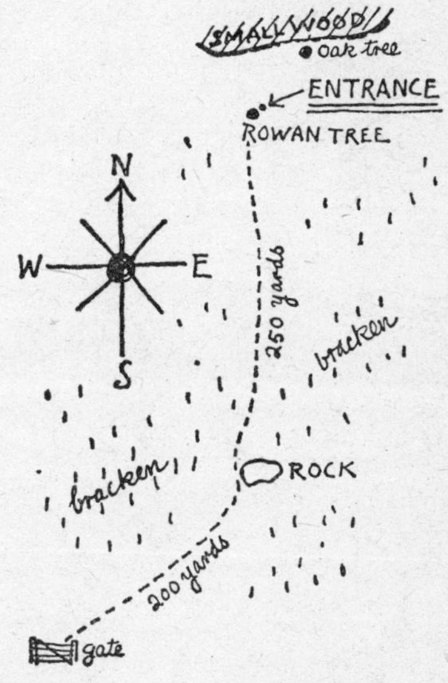

with the drawing-block on his knees. First he marked the position of the central rock, then of the field gate and of the rowan tree. With these cardinal points he felt his way by careful measurements until the whole sketch map was complete. He was rather proud of it and almost regretted that if the expedition should be successfully carried out, nobody would see the map. On second thoughts, however, he decided that at the end of the holiday he would be able to give the map to his uncle, thus in some measure to show

how much he appreciated the attitude of the doctor towards the members of the Tomahawk Club.

With this reflection he finished the job and made the return journey across the sea of bracken. The wind, meanwhile, had dropped and once more an evening sun shone upon the green expanse. All was calm and still, and the mists had disappeared. The berries on the rowan tree not only burned but blazed. The rocks and the hills beyond them were outlined sharply against the blue sky. Time stood still, waiting for great events.

CHAPTER 5

A DIPLOMATIC DINNER

THE result of Aunt Mary's suggestion was that on Tuesday evening at a quarter to seven, George Reynolds, in a clean but tooth-edged collar, presented himself at the doctor's house. He was waylaid in the hall by his fellow-conspirator, who drew him into the cloakroom.

'Look here,' said John, 'I don't know why she's asked you but I suspect a trap. She's out for information, so watch your step. We don't want to be stopped at the last moment. If she gets wind of it she may telephone round to all our people. She is a terror for anticipating trouble. I suppose it's because she once worked in a hospital.'

This warning appeared to give no surprise to George. He inserted his finger between his raw neck and the wicked edge of his collar and tried in vain to ease the situation. But here again he adopted his habitual air of resignation.

'I thought so,' he said, 'you can't be offered a treat like this without there being a snag in it. I've kept out of the way at home today. If you're not seen, you're forgotten. That's how things work at our place, especially when there's a crisis on.' Then he added sadly, 'And there's always a crisis on in our home.'

This unusual confidence seemed to fill him with remorse and he entered the dining-room looking more depressed than ever. Aunt Mary was setting a jar of chrysanthemums in the middle of the table which was laid with her best china. Instead of shaking hands with her nephew's guest, she stood holding the flowers in front of her and looked at him over them.

'Do you think they are the right colour, George?' And she studied him earnestly.

George's lack-lustre eyes suddenly lit up as he contemplated the great mops of gold and purple glowing under the lamplight. 'My word!' was all he said.

John looked at him in surprise. This was not the George Reynolds of the boat-house and the daily adventures along the riverside. Here was a boy really excited at last by something which couldn't be explained. It seemed that Aunt Mary knew how to read people. The realization made John uneasy. If his aunt was determined to find things out, what was to prevent her? He was powerless, and he contemplated an evening in which he and George would be led to betray the secrets of the Tomahawk Club, and thus to earn the contempt of its other members.

These misgivings, however, were thrust aside when the doctor came in wiping his hands on a face towel. He said nothing, but clapped George on the back and nodded at his nephew with an assumption of ferocity.

'Early for once, my dear,' he said, pointing with his nose at George Reynolds, 'in honour of our guest.' He rolled the towel up into a ball and threw it into an armchair, whence his wife demurely rescued it, and used it to wipe a rim of moisture from the base of the flower vase as she placed it on the table.

'Feeling fine, Reynolds?' he asked, 'or are you running to fat?'

He dug the thin, lugubrious figure in the ribs. Then he poured out four glasses of sherry, and offered one first to his wife and then handed the tray to the boys. 'People of an enterprising nature deserve something to comfort them,' he said.

Two suspicious minds at once leapt to the alarm, but instantly John was ashamed of himself. One look at his uncle's face, a mask of bland innocence, reassured him. Here at last was no sign of a conspiracy of grown-ups to keep the Tomahawk Club from its dangerous adventure next morning.

As the meal proceeded, George Reynolds came still farther out of his shell. The pale face took on a tinge of colour and the dull eyes a spark of fire. Something about Aunt Mary had stirred his gloomy mind, and John saw him looking at her from time to time in a way that was almost worship, if George was capable of worship. It seemed, too, that Aunt Mary knew what she was doing and was determined to make the most of it, for she addressed herself almost entirely to her young visitor, serving him first and piling his plate with food enough for two. The result was that the silent George began to talk. His croaking voice, usually like that of a moulting raven, rose and fell, broke and regathered itself as he was delivered of what were, for him, long outbursts of speech.

'It must be dull for you,' said Aunt Mary, as she helped him to a second plateful of chocolate pudding, 'to have to stay at home throughout the summer holidays. Whatever have you done with yourself?'

'I don't grumble,' he said. 'I don't find time drag, for there's plenty to see.'

'See?' exclaimed the doctor, who had been consuming his meal silently in a business-like way. 'So you like looking at things, do you, Reynolds? Got a pair of eyes in your head, have you?'

George turned that pair of eyes upon the doctor, and was groping about for words to reply when the conversation was interrupted by a ring at the doorbell. A moment later, Alan Hobbs was shown into the dining-room. He was not embarrassed although he could see that he was disturbing the household at dinner. He walked up and shook the doctor by the hand and the latter looked at him rather bleakly. Even this, however, did not reduce him, and he turned to Aunt Mary with a smile on his handsome face.

'I thought John might have an hour to spare,' he said, 'we want to make the most of the last two weeks of the holidays. Things are always rather flat after you get home, especially if you've been abroad. I've just got back from Switzerland. Have you ever been there, Dr Walters?'

The doctor swallowed, put his napkin down on the tablecloth and looked at Alan for some moments in silence. John could see his eyes glinting in the subdued light of the shaded lamps. 'Yes,' he said thoughtfully, 'I have been to Switzerland quite a bit in my time. And what did you do there, Hobbs?' This question provoked the boy to a wonderful story about his exploits in the Alps and among the mountain lakes. John listened with envy, staring at this brilliant friend spellbound. George sat with downcast eyes; the veil of gloom once more dropped over his face.

The discourse was suddenly interrupted by an abrupt movement from the doctor, who rose from the table and somewhat rudely ignored the heroic tale which Alan was building up over a plate of chocolate pudding which Aunt Mary had thrust upon him.

'Well,' said the doctor, turning his back on Alan and addressing himself to George. 'I must go over and pay my respects to a young member who is just about to enter this world. I am glad to know you've got the habit of looking about you, Reynolds. You can learn a lot that way. It's often better than blowing off steam.'

He walked out of the room without further comment, ignoring everybody else. John was puzzled, for he recognized that his uncle only behaved like this when he was angry about something, and surely tonight nothing had happened to rouse the doctor in that way, unless he was bored by George coming to supper, and was annoyed because Aunt Mary had made so much fuss of the fellow who was a next-door neighbour and a member of a large and chaotic household.

At any rate, he thought it wise now to remove both his friends before further harm was done, so asking his aunt's permission he took them up to his room where they could talk without being overheard.

It was a warm night and he flung open both casement windows, calling his friends to look out with him. The three boys stood there in silence, staring at a landscape bewitched by moonlight. The garden below was an unrecognizable mass of lights and shadows, which concealed fruit trees, lawns and flower borders. The copse beyond the garden, that stretched into the Reynolds' property, now hung in space, a depth of darkness out of which at any moment something vivid might flash. From time to time a leaf fluttered or a bough stirred, and immediately a flicker of silver fire tumbled out of that dark body.

Beyond the chimney-tops of George's home, which appeared above the trees, a faint gleam showed the hills, flattened under the moonlight into streaks of lead, half polished and half tarnished. The air was warm and very still; a smell of autumn rose from the earth, mouldy, fruitful.

John heard George draw a deep breath and saw him lean forward with hands on the sill, so that the moonlight fell across his face. Once again that evening John stared at a friend transfigured. He was still wondering about this when Alan Hobbs broke the spell.

'Oh, boy!' he said, 'I could hardly keep myself in check before your aunt and uncle. I almost gave the game away. The point is that I've borrowed my father's lamp.'

'What reason did you give him?' said George.

'There was no need to give a reason. I did not think it worth while to mention the matter. There's no harm done in borrowing it for he doesn't use it except on winter nights when he's putting the Bentley away. I found it in the gun-room and all I needed to do was to put a new battery in. My father always keeps a few spare ones.' He reflected for a few moments, then added as he switched on the light without asking permission, 'It's a pity about that compass which Lightning is bringing. We ought to have something really reliable, you know. It ought to be a prismatic. I don't like leading an expedition that isn't properly equipped. After all, it's a big responsibility.'

George again said nothing and turned once more to contemplate the scene of the moonlit world outside. John quietly reassured Alan and said that he thought it possible that he might borrow a larger compass from his uncle who had been a mountaineer.

'A mountaineer?' said Alan, with rising excitement. 'Then I must have made his mouth water when I was talking about my holiday in Switzerland!'

CHAPTER 6

FOLLOW MY LEADER

AT nine o'clock on the Wednesday morning, each member of the Tomahawk Club slipped away from home as discreetly as possible, with his contribution to the equipment of the exploration party hidden under his mackintosh. Odd bulges and bumps might have led to some inquiry if the members had been seen by grown-ups; but all five boys were expert in the art of disappearing from the family circle with a minimum of fuss. Not one of them was stopped that morning, and within five minutes of leaving their homes they were all converging safely towards the rock in the middle of the field of bracken, the appointed meeting place.

John and George met in the road outside their homes, and went together. It had been laid down that mackintoshes were to be worn in order to cover the ropes, axes and all the rest of the stuff commandeered for the occasion. George managed to conform only by commandeering a mackintosh also. It was borrowed from an older brother and hung about his lank form, almost touching the ground. It would have done so had it not been supported from within by the various objects which he brought with him.

The sight was so comic that John, seeing him emerge from the tumble-down gate of the next-door house, could not hide a grin of amusement. George, preoccupied with the anxiety of escaping from a house in which nobody had any privacy, looked more lugubrious than ever. He noticed the smile which greeted him and his dull eyes gleamed with a good-humoured reflection of his friend's mirth.

'Phew,' he breathed, 'I had a job to get away with all this clobber,' and he looked down at his distended figure as though he could not believe it to be true.

The friends hurried down the road out of the town and were soon in open country, much to their relief. It was not easy going, for the sun was already warm on their faces and their burdens were heavy.

'What on earth have you got there?' said John, nudging one of the larger promontories under George's mackintosh. This familiarity upset the delicate balance of George's superstructure, and the whole protrusion dropped, almost throwing him over as it fell about his feet. Even this, however, did not move him to ill-humour. Nor did it make him smile.

'It's a rope ladder,' he said, 'I spent yesterday making it up from all the odd pieces of rope in our boat-house. I know it's strong because I've often helped the fishermen down on the beach and learned how to make knots and do splicing. It's not very long but I think it's got a drop of twenty feet. That may be useful.'

While saying this, he had been standing with knees bent, groping on the ground for the ladder while trying to keep himself upright in order to avoid more disasters. This was too much for John, who was really excited with the sense of adventure and the successful way in which everything appeared to be working out. He roared with laughter and only with difficulty managed to extricate his neighbour from the coiled-up ladder which he proceeded to carry himself.

'My word,' he said, 'you've put some work into this.'

'Oh, I don't know,' grunted the other, unused to praise. 'We want to do the thing properly.'

They went on without more mishap and reached the gate leading into the bracken, where they paused to get their breath. The slanting sunlight was dazzlingly bright in their eyes and every tree and bush stood haloed with a nimbus of fire that danced with morning joy. There was no wind, and a number of swifts darted about over the bracken like skaters on a pond, sometimes approaching so near to the boys they could hear the thrust of their wings and the little twittering cries of the hunting birds.

The rock stood up in the level sunshine like a miniature Gibraltar. On its flat top, a small figure sat cross-legged. It was Harold Soames, who, true to his character, was the first to arrive. He saw them standing at the gate, jumped up and began to dance and wave his arms, not so much to greet them, as to get rid of some of his excess of energy and joy of life. They plunged through the bracken and when they reached the rock, John hurled the rope ladder like a lasso

He jumped up and began to dance and wave his arms

at the gesticulating figure and managed to bring him to his knees.

'Brute!' he gasped, his piercing voice more shrill than ever. Then he shouted, 'We're on our way; we're on our way into the bowels of the earth,' and began to dance again.

'Don't be an idiot,' said John, 'you don't want to tell the whole world, after all our efforts to keep quiet.'

At this moment, the party was joined by Meaty Sanders and Alan Hobbs, both dressed according to the book in mackintosh, over sweater and shorts. The Tomahawk Club

Five boys dropped from the rock and walked in Indian file

now being fully assembled, an inquiry into procedure was held. Alan quickly reassumed direction of affairs and began by ordering the members, one by one, to produce their contributions to the expedition. George had to show not only his rope ladder, but a hammer, cold chisel, the big ball of tarred twine, three candles and a box of matches, and the picnic basket.

'Where's your torch?' said Alan, severely.

A look of utmost gloom spread over George's face, and he turned his head from side to side as though seeking to hide it in shame. Then, from under his mackintosh, he slowly produced the dark-lantern which had been so scornfully rejected the day before. But now it was clean and polished and ready for action.

'I am sorry I couldn't get a torch,' he said, 'things are a bit muddled at our place.'

Alan did not even bother to look at the lantern. He turned to the others inquiringly, like a judge addressing the jury.

'What do you say to that?' he asked. Then relenting somewhat, he added, 'Well, I suppose we must let it go.'

George appeared to find this leniency even more crushing than the rebuke, for he turned aside as though to leave the expedition.

'I don't know,' interrupted John, 'we've got torches and candles. A third source of light may be the saving of us. Anything may happen underground.'

'Third,' sneered Alan, 'you call that smelly old antique a source of light! Why do we want to carry that sort of thing when I've brought *this*.'

With a gesture of authority he flung off his mackintosh which had been carried over his shoulders. In his hand was a magnificent instrument. It was his father's electric lamp with a flat lens in front and a great bull's eye on top. It was made of metal protected with hoops, one of which swung as a handle. Everybody stared at it in admiration, and little Harold, in his eagerness, stretched a hand to touch it.

'No, you don't,' said Alan, knocking the hand aside, 'I borrowed this without asking; so no meddling. I'm in charge of this, whatever happens, so long as I'm leading the expedition.'

Nobody questioned this claim and after further exclamations of wonder and praise of the glory of the lamp, business was resumed. Nobody commented on the fact that the lamp was Alan's sole contribution. He had not even brought food and drink with him, but this was counter-weighted by the contents of a rucksack which Meaty Sanders unloaded. His father kept a big general store in the middle of the town, and the son had been able to gather the crumbs from beneath that table. There was three-quarters of a veal pie wrapped in grease-proof paper. There was a length of cooked sausage, a large lump of cheese, a loaf of bread and half a pound of margarine, with several packets of made sandwiches. He dived into the sack again and produced a tin of salmon, a tin of peaches and a bag of tomatoes. He had even thought to bring a tin-opener. Finally, he held up two bottles, one of lemonade and the other of orange. Meaty stared at his own larder and his protruding eyes glistened with satisfaction.

'We ought to be all right,' he said, numbering the articles one by one.

The general agreement with this statement was so hearty that no one thought to inquire why Alan Hobbs had failed to bring anything whatever. After all, the fellow who had brought the lamp was a law unto himself, and was in a position to ignore Napoleon's statement that an army marched on its belly.

Harold's turn came next. With a slight air of disgust, he produced three packets wrapped in paper napkins and tied with coloured raffia. It was the wrapping that disgusted him, not the contents.

'I said we were going for a picnic,' he explained, 'and the sisters did this for me.' There was a plaintive note in his voice, as he touched one of the dainty little bows with the tip of a grubby finger. 'And they made me bring a hot drink.' He showed a thermos flask and a bottle of milk at the other end of his neat little satchel. His mood changed, however, when he took out for the second time, his pocket compass. He had forgotten Alan's criticism, for it was not in his nature to be subdued for long. 'We shall want this,' he said, pointing to it with emphasis, and this time Alan had nothing further to say. Nor did John, but he put a thumb and finger into the little pocket on the belt of his shorts in order to reassure himself about a matter which he preferred not to disclose at that stage of the day's events.

It was now John's turn to declare. He showed his uncle's hundred-foot mountaineer's rope, carefully coiled and tied with string; then he produced his own ten-inch torch, spare battery and bulb. He did not reveal the fact that the little pocket pencil torch belonging to his uncle, also complete with extra battery, was stowed in his hip pocket, but he did produce from that pocket a first-aid box. With this he had a confession to make.

'Look here,' he said, 'you fellows had better know that my uncle found out about our plan, but you can be sure we can rely on him not to say anything. He said I was to bring this with me, and when I went to look for it in the hall as I came out this morning, I also found this parcel.' He then unloaded from his own rucksack a substantial package wrapped in a tea-cloth and fastened with a huge safety pin.

He never doubted that this was also part of his uncle's work.

'That looks good,' said Meaty. 'Do you know what's in it?'

'No,' said John, somewhat abruptly, thrusting the parcel back beside his water flask. 'It's time we got going.'

Alan took up his suggestion instantly, even anxiously.

'Come along, now,' he cried, assuming that the suggestion had been his, 'Pack your things and you lead the way, John. I'll take over when we get inside.'

Five boys dropped from the rock and walked in Indian file towards the rowan tree. Each carried his own gear and also a stick to grope the way.

'Here we are,' said John, carefully dividing the bracken without beating it down from the front of the hole. 'We mustn't disturb the entrance or someone may discover it. It's one at a time now until we get past the drop. We've still to explore that. I've no idea what lies beyond, or how deep the drop may be. It means crawling along the tunnel and one of us going down after we've looked round with a light.'

'A light?' queried Alan. 'Then I'd better lead the way. Don't you agree?'

Nobody disagreed, so Alan went down on his hands and knees and was the first to enter the tunnel. The others followed him. The bracken closed over the mouth of the cave and the sun shone on the rock and the rowan tree. There was no sign of humanity on the earth's surface.

CHAPTER 7

A TIGHT SQUEEZE

At first, the change from the dazzling sunlight to the darkness of the tunnel made the glow of three pocket torches feeble. But even so Alan preserved his lamp. It was too important to be used at the beginning of the adventure. He directed John, immediately behind him, to show a light over his shoulder so that he could see his way. This John did with his ten-inch torch, throwing a beam which steadily became more revealing as the boys' eyes grew accustomed to the underground world. John could feel Lightning Soames pushing him from behind, but he could not increase his pace because Alan was moving with careful deliberation, feeling his way foot by foot, with the stick out-thrust just as John himself had done when discovering the cave. John was compelled to admire the methodical way in which the leader of the expedition was setting out.

Alan had now reached the end of the tunnel entrance, and he paused for a moment before entering the deeper slope of the passage, at the end of which lay the unknown.

'Did you get as far as this?' he asked, over his shoulder.

'Yes,' said John, 'it leads to the drop, and that's where I had to stop. It was impossible without a torch, and maybe we shall need a ladder or a rope.'

'Good,' said the leader. 'Keep the light over my shoulder. Now for it!'

With that he began to crawl down the shaft, forgetting to issue instructions to the rest of the party. Before following him, John turned to the other three boys and told them to halt, explaining that the passage narrowed and that there would be no room for them with all their clobber until further knowledge had been obtained of the formation of the chimney where it gave into the open space beyond. The three boys somewhat timidly agreed to this; nervous at being left in the tunnel while the two more responsible members disappeared from sight.

Alan crawled down the shaft to the narrow part where John's coat had been pulled up round him in his first effort to beat a retreat. Both boys had already shed their burdens.

'I shall have to use my lamp now,' he shouted. 'You can't get your light past me, can you?'

His voice was already muffled as though he were speaking with his head in a box. John directed his torch light, but all he could see was the soles of Alan's shoes and the seat of his shorts which entirely filled the tunnel. He could do no more for the moment, and had to wait while Alan wriggled forward like a terrier thrusting into a rabbit hole. Suddenly, the feet and legs shot forward convulsively. He had broken through to the little funnel-shaped expansion which opened on the unknown abyss, or whatever might lie beyond. John heard him breathing vigorously and a few words came floating back.

'I'm through,' gasped Alan.

After a few moments pause, during which John could see flashes of light through the small gaps between Alan's body and the walls of the tunnel, he shouted again, and this time his breath was more under control.

'There's a ledge, John. It's about three feet below us. If we get down to it, I think we can walk round to a wide platform on the left. It's a sort of balcony, but I can't see any way down from it yet. It looks safe enough from here, anyway, so we had better tell the others to follow up and push our gear through. You call them and I'll get down to the ledge, then you can follow me and we can help them down.'

John crept backwards as instructed and told the other three what was to be done next. He then returned down the tunnel, followed by Lightning, who was babbling with excitement, and because of his small size was able to make light work of the difficulties due to the narrowing of the passage.

John worked his way through the narrow neck and lay on his stomach in the funnel-opening, gazing into space. This time, however, he had his torch, and there below him was Alan throwing the mighty beam of his electric lamp back towards him.

'You're dazzling my eyes!' shouted John. 'Turn it down so that we can see what's below.'

It was impossible, however, for Alan to do what he was asked without first putting up some show of independence. He threw the beam of his lamp outwards and upwards, and the great shaft went searching round, prodding its way, yard by yard, over the broken surface of what proved to be a cavern of impressive size. The funnel through which the boys had entered it, was about three-quarters of the way up, thus leaving them with head room of about twenty feet, and a drop (so far as John could see by the light of his own torch) of some fifty feet.

The silence was uncanny. A faint scrambling sound behind them indicated that the other boys were making their way down the funnel and would at any moment be appearing like small white maggots. The silence in the cavern itself was so intense that the shaft of light from Alan's lamp seemed definitely to make a noise as it hit the walls with its circular blunted end, a flat ring about three feet in diameter. This medallion of light crept systematically over the roof of the cavern at the dictate of Alan's will directing his hand on the lamp. The sight was so fascinating that John still had not further examined the depth below, nor had he made any movement to get out of the mouth of the tunnel on to the ledge. There he lay, on his stomach, with his head thrown back, staring upwards at the explorations of the electric beam. Suddenly, its movements stopped and both boys gazed awestricken at a vast cleft in the centre of the vault. It spread almost from one side to the other and then ended abruptly in a huge boss of rock which appeared to be hanging like a gigantic chandelier with nothing to support it. This pear-shaped rock glistened when the beam struck it, and the boys could see a trickle of moisture seeping through what appeared to be the sandy softness of its outer surface. From its lower lobe hung a huge stalk. It was a stalactite, formed by the water that found its way from the upper earth down through the giant fissure and gathered round the rock before dripping through the cave with that faint clock-like tick-tock which John had heard when he first explored on the Sunday evening. This gigantic needle shone flesh-coloured in the artificial light, and the water trickling down it gave the effect of a blood-stream within, or of the movement of muscles beneath the skin of a white human arm.

The boys were so startled by this apparition in the roof that they stared at it and forgot their former desire to look round the rest of the cave. They forgot also the companions who were following them, but this matter was quickly remedied by a hand that seized John's foot and shook it impatiently. Recalled to himself, he wriggled round until he was sitting on the edge of the funnel and could drop to the ledge below. He was instantly followed by Lightning, for Lightning worked that way. The little figure bounced out of the narrow neck like a ball from a cup, and at once began to ask questions.

'What's that over there?' he demanded, 'How far does it go down?' And then when he had looked up along the beam and saw the rock hanging out of the cleft, and the living stalactite, he crowed with excitement, crying: 'Oh look, look at that! Is it going to fall?'

John put a restraining hand on his shoulder.

'Be careful,' he said. 'Sometimes it is dangerous to shout in places like this. The least vibration can over-balance a weight that has been trembling on the brink for a thousand years.'

This statement amused Alan, and he at once started to put it to the test, or perhaps to defy it. 'Ooh,' he shouted, throwing back his head and bellowing like a bull. He repeated the noise and glared defiantly at John. The sides of the cavern caught the sound, beat it like a red-hot iron, until it became hard and dangerous, and then flung it up for the third time, reinforced by a cluster of echoes, towards the roof. There the sound broke up, shattered itself and was about to die away when, suddenly, there was a crack, and a shadow dropped out of the fissure in the roof, followed by a waft of dank-smelling air. The listeners heard a heavy splash below, a broken noise of weltering water. Then silence filled the cave once more. The whole incident might have been a delusion.

'What was that?' whispered Lightning, his voice trembling a little.

'It must have been a fall of rock,' said John, and his voice too was hushed to a whisper. 'All that damp stuff there in the cleft where the water is trickling through must be half rotten, and it looks as though there is nothing to hold it except the pressure from the sides. We'd better be careful, Alan.'

But Alan did not reply. He had switched off the mighty beam of his father's lamp and stood in darkness and silence. John hesitated. He was angry, for he resented the lack of confidence in the sense of teamwork; but he did not find the words to express himself. For one thing, he feared that he might make Alan quarrelsome and so break up the day's adventure, and that was the last thing he wanted to do. While he was deciding therefore to say nothing, and to leave Alan still in command, the incident was temporarily forgotten because real trouble had begun. Meaty Sanders was stuck in the funnel. They heard him groaning and puffing as he struggled to break through the neck, but at last he had to call out in a half-strangled voice.

Alan immediately took command of the situation. Handing his lamp to John, he instructed him to shine it back up the funnel so that he could see what was best to do. With that, he scrambled up from the ledge and made his way to the boy's head and shoulders, stuck into the mouth of the funnel out of the bottle-neck.

'Don't move for a minute,' he said, 'I'm thinking what to do.' Before he had thought to any purpose, however, Meaty, aided by George from behind, began to withdraw like a tube train disappearing out of the station. As he went, the worried look left his face, and it was a cheerful grin that finally disappeared out of the beam of light into the darkness of the passage.

They heard his shout: 'I'm all right, but how am I to get through?'

It was John who answered, and in his excitement he had forgotten his own advice about raising one's voice. He shouted cheerily from the ledge, 'You'll have to undress and leave all your luggage behind and try again.' His voice set the echoes dancing again round the walls and up to the roof of the cavern, but this time nothing happened. Meanwhile, Meaty had taken his advice literally, and a few moments later the head and shoulders of the fat boy reappeared, and with greater determination. He struggled and sweated until his eyes bulged even more than was usual above his massive cheeks. He clenched his teeth and thrust forward again. Alan knelt down and took him under the shoulders, pulling until Meaty cried out in pain. By this time, John had joined Alan in the funnel and was throwing a flood of light on the situation with the aid of the lamp.

'Don't just struggle blindly,' he said. 'Breathe out as much as you can and wriggle forward while there is no breath in your body. You must be some inches smaller like that.'

This advice proved to be sound. Meaty repeated the experiment again and again, and each time worked his stout body an inch or two farther through the narrow passage.

The sweat trickled down his face, but he could not bring up an arm to clear his eyes.

'How am I going to get back?' he spluttered; but there was not much fear in the inquiry, for he was grinning once more, confident that having moved so far, he would soon be through. So it proved. A few more exhalations of breath, the technique being the opposite to that of a deep-sea diver, a few more rests during which John wiped his face with a handkerchief, and at last Meaty squeezed through and dropped to the ledge, dressed in his skin. They examined him by the light of the lamp and found him none the worse except for some rough patches on his tummy and a couple of grazed knees and elbows. His eyes looked a little bloodshot, but all he said was 'My word! that's made me hungry.'

George had now pushed his face through the bottle-neck and followed up with the ample larder which Meaty had provided. By the time Meaty had dressed, George was through the funnel, and little Lightning had gone up again to fetch the odds and ends of apparatus and stores which had been left in the level part of the passage. At that stage, Meaty insisted upon some refreshment for his outraged digestive system. He also insisted that the whole party should eat from his supply. 'It'll all be the same by the day's end,' he said, energetically unpacking the top layers of his large rucksack and producing cucumber sandwiches and a packet of Pat-a-cake biscuits. The Tomahawk Club, strung out in a line on the ledge, squatted on their heels, eating by the light of the noble lamp set down beside their leader. Nobody spoke; nothing moved, except five pairs of jaws munching. Along the front of the crouching boys stood the beam of light, like a hand-rail. Beyond it lay darkness, massive, shapeless.

CHAPTER 8

FEAR

It was that darkness which put an end to the comfortable interval for food. Gradually, the munching ceased and all five boys knew that the moment had come to step out on the next stage of the adventure.

Alan began by jumping to his feet, picking up his lamp and, for the first time, sending its beam to the floor of the cavern. Everybody shrank back, for not until now had they realized that they were perched up on this narrow ridge close to the roof of the underground cathedral. The beam moved about, searching the floor and showing it littered with rocks of various sizes. Here was evidence of those periodic falls of which they had witnessed an example a few minutes ago. The boys were too high up to see much in detail, but even from their ledge they could be sure that some of the rocks had fallen more recently, because they were still raw and sharp edged. Others carried quilts of vegetation that looked like camel cloths.

In the centre of the floor, directly beneath the great stalactite, lay a heart-shaped mass, darker than its surroundings. Alan directed and steadied the beam on to it. Suddenly it shivered. Another drop had fallen from seventy feet above; deep, ominous, slow. All five gazed in awe, and a few moments later they saw and heard a repetition of that solemn measurement of time.

'It's water,' said Lightning, 'let's go and explore.'

'Idiot,' said Meaty, amiably. He was a person who could say the most crushing things without ever hurting anybody's feelings. 'Do you think we are going to fly down? Like bats?'

'We've got a rope, haven't we?' said Lightning.

John interrupted. 'Yes,' he said, 'but we don't want to use it over this sharp edge unless we're driven to it. It might be a good idea to carry on along the ledge on the left to see that spot where –'

'I know,' Alan butted in. 'That's what I planned. We'll see what this wide platform means. There may be a way down from it. But you must follow me carefully because it slopes a little and a slip might be bad.'

'I'm certain it would,' said John. 'If you look closely you see not only that it slopes down to the platform but it's also got a tilt outward; and that makes for treacherous footing. We can't risk anything, so we must rope ourselves together like mountaineers.'

Alan again insisted on leading, so he was the first to have the rope tied round his waist. It was then paid out six feet and secured round Lightning. Next in the chain came Meaty. He was followed by George and John was last man. Each took up his burden and the crocodile began to move, step by step, the footholds being picked out by Alan's lamp, three torches and–a dark-lantern.

While George produced matches and lit the lantern, nobody said a word, for they all understood why he had to bring it. A loud sniff from Alan was the only comment; sufficient to show his authority. The lantern stank for a few moments and smoke poured from it, but George turned down the wick and the red flame brightened into a warm glow that in comparison with the glare of the torches, shone like a ripe orange. At the same time, it suggested reliability, and at least three of the other members of the club felt the more comfortable for its existence.

The explorers soon discovered how necessary the rope could be, for they had not made more than half the distance towards the platform when Lightning slipped, lost his footing and would have slid over the edge had not the rope brought him up sharp and enabled him to cling on his hands and knees. This made everybody a little shaky.

'Take it easy there,' boomed George.

'Good thing it wasn't me,' said Meaty; but his voice broke into a girlish treble, 'My weight would have brought you all down.'

The boy who had fallen said nothing. He was angry with himself, thinking he had been childish: and that was the last thing he wanted to be.

The boys crept on more cautiously now, treading their way, inch by inch. The ledge sloped more dangerously as they proceeded, until at last they were brought to a standstill because the foothold had crumbled into a mass of loose shale, leaving the firm part only about twelve inches wide. That too, had to be cleared of debris before they dared tread on it. This broken surface stretched for about twelve feet, and beyond it, the ledge resumed its firm surface, rapidly widening as it approached the platform.

The problem now was how to cross this intervening twelve feet of treachery.

'Let me think,' said Alan, raking with his stick at the nearest of the loose stuff on the crumbled ledge, and sending it rustling down to the floor of the cave. Some of it was so thin that it went flying like bats in the darkness. 'I'm going to unrope and go on alone,' he said.

Everybody was impressed by this foolhardiness. Even while he spoke, however, his voice trailed away into silence without being followed by action. He was waiting for something, and John supplied it.

'You can't do that,' said John. 'Those of us who are wearing leather shoes must take them off and we must cross in our socks. George is all right because he is wearing gym. shoes. We must tie our shoes round our necks and put them on again when we get to firm ground. Take care that your rucksacks don't catch on the wall, test each step as you go. There are good handholds to steady yourselves.'

Alan was so relieved at not having to carry out his own proposal, that he raised no further objection. In a few minutes shoes were off and tied by their laces round the owner's necks; packs were adjusted and the human train crawled forward. To the delight of everybody, the foothold that had seemed so dangerous now proved to be firm. The safe part of the ledge was reached, the boys unroped, breathed freely and put on their shoes again.

'That makes me feel hungry,' said Meaty for the second time, but he was hustled forward and not allowed to stop for refreshment.

It was discovered that two of the company had left their sticks behind, but no one suggested recrossing the danger spot to recover them. The next stretch was easy going with the ledge broadening and rising to the platform, which appeared to be a perfect horizontal floor, forming a balcony wide enough to support a house.

Everybody sighed with relief, although none of the boys would have admitted, even to himself, that the last few minutes while crossing the faulty rock face had been a hair-raising experience. They peered over the edge of the platform and found they were standing on the flat top of a vast pillar of rock which went down, thinner and thinner, to the floor of the cavern. Its sides shrank quickly from the top to a narrow waist. The explorers were thus standing on a fan-shaped shelf, sticking out about forty feet from the wall of the cavern which curved over their heads towards the centre of the roof.

'Keep away from the edge,' said George, 'It looks brittle to me.'

Alan stood back and poked at the extreme edge with his stick, proving that George's pessimism was for once justified. A great bite was taken out of the edge and the detached piece of rock hit the floor of the cave minutes later, as it seemed to the listeners.

'I told you so,' said Alan, and nobody cared to contradict him, for he appeared to be so sure that the warning had come from him.

The increased space and freedom made the darkness only the more impenetrable, and the farther reaches of the platform were hidden even when every member of the party turned his light in that direction. The obvious thing was to explore there, to search for a possible outlet that might lead down to the pool below.

When people are excited, however, they do not always do the obvious thing. The bright beam from the leader's lamp moved round the interior of the platform, and suddenly there was a cry from Alan: 'Look! Look! There's an opening.' Once again he ran forward, forgetting the rest of the company.

This time they followed him more closely, and all five boys found themselves confronting an archway as large as a church door, and about the same shape. They peered through it and then entered boldly, discovering that they were passing through a rift in a wall of rock about ten feet thick. Beyond this, the sides opened out like those of a large well, while the ceiling remained about seven or eight feet above their heads. After the excitement and babble of the voices had died down, the boys were surprised to find that the silence of the great cavern had not followed them into this interior chamber.

Far below them, a curious ticking sound was heard. As their ears became accustomed to this sound, it sorted itself out and, beneath that periodical tap, tap they heard a steady but hushed murmur.

Once more the big lamp came into action. The confined space made its beam all the brighter, and five white faces shone in the sepulchral light. The boys could see themselves looking at each other with eagerness.

'It's down below,' said Meaty, and his great, strong body leaned forward as he flashed his torch to the spot where he thought he identified the sound. Alan followed suit, and the boys found themselves staring down the pot-hole, the bottom of which defied the beams of light from the torches.

From time to time there seemed to be a gleam, a faint flicker thrown up from what must be the bottom, but it appeared to be much deeper than the floor of the great cavern. The temperature too, was different. The faces peering into the depth felt a deathly chill that touched their skins as though with fingers of frost. An odour of cold steel came up from the deep. Any explorer might be forgiven a spasm of fear before deciding to venture further. Lightning, however, had no such misgivings.

'Who's going down?' he piped, his voice as shrill as ever. 'I'll go, if you like.'

None of the others backed his proposal. They flashed their torches down, seeking more information before making any suggestions.

'It's a river,' said John. 'I'm certain of it. What I don't understand is why it isn't flowing through the main shaft. Perhaps one of those great falls of rock from the roof may have blocked the stream some time or other, and it has eaten its way through flaws in the solid rock round the sides of the cave. If so, it must be flowing towards the other end of the cave, and we may have entered from somewhere near the back.'

'Yes,' growled George, who stood behind his dark-lantern like an old-fashioned night watchman. 'With the stream running that way, it must flow as a tributary of the main river, joining it near the bend round the end of the hills.'

'Well,' said Lightning, piping up again, 'if it flows on, there must be an opening; and if there's an opening, then it's safe for us to go down and look for it. I'm willing enough.' And he danced with excitement. It was impossible to ignore him, for his eagerness was catching, and Meaty was the next to volunteer.

'I'll go down the rope,' he said, making motions with his arms like a sailor dancing a hornpipe. Everybody laughed, and all fear of danger was forgotten.

John, meanwhile, had been examining the edge over which the rope would have to be paid out. He selected the smoothest part and proceeded to hammer the two cold chisels into the floor of the rock close to the wall at about two feet apart.

'We'll pay out the rope round those,' he said, kicking them sharply to make sure that they were secure and would bear a boy's weight. Then he tied the inner end of his uncle's mountaineering rope to one of the chisels, which now acted as pegs, and paid out the other end, carrying it to the edge of the pot-hole.

'Now,' he said, 'we must decide who is to go down.' He looked to Alan Hobbs, who had become silent and withdrawn. There was a pause, and Alan knew that he was expected to take the lead again and to make this important decision. Suddenly he became reckless.

'Why, we'll all go,' he cried.

John replied quietly, 'We can hardly do that. It needs three to take charge of the rope at this end.'

'And suppose there's no way out at the bottom,' said George. 'How should we get up again? It would mean a search party finding five white skeletons in a few months' time.'

This amused Meaty, and his huge frame could be seen quivering with mirth in the dim light of the torches.

'Yes, that's what I mean,' said Alan. 'We want to explore first, of course. Well, you and young Lightning had better go,' he said to John.

John said no more but tied the rope securely round his waist, took the rope ladder, tied it also to the iron pegs, and laid it as a carpet and buffer between the rope and the rock edge.

'Let me down gradually,' he said, 'and pay out the rope over the rope ladder so that it does not fray against the rock. When I touch bottom I'll give two tugs; but don't haul the rope up until I repeat the two tugs. Three tugs will mean that I am in difficulties and you must haul me back; but again, don't do it in a hurry.'

He was glad to notice that George Reynolds had stepped back, put down his dark-lantern on a ledge, and was now writing these instructions on the corner of a small drawing-block, mysteriously produced for the first time.

'Somebody might forget,' he muttered. 'Just as well to make sure.'

'But can't I go down first?' cried Lightning, and he seized the rope round John's waist.

'No,' said John. 'I brought this rope and I must make sure that it is safe. If it will bear my weight, it'll carry a shrimp like you.'

Lightning almost cried with rage. Anything resembling the protective kindness and coddling with which he was mothered at home always had this effect. Here, however, Alan reasserted his authority.

'That's enough,' he said, in a loud clear voice. The commotion subsided, and was followed by action.

John divested himself of all his equipment except the small torch and compass in his pockets, and candle and matches, and the ten-inch torch which he had tied round his waist with string. He switched this on and let himself down over the edge. The careful control of the rope by the other boys, with George and Meaty paying it out, ensured a steady descent. Foot by foot, yard by yard, he was lowered into the darkness. The light from the torch round his waist veered wildly as he swung and began to turn like a joint on a spit. He felt himself growing giddy, and put out a foot to steady himself against the wall of the pot-hole. But he could not reach it, for the space was widening as he went down and he found himself hanging more and more in what seemed to him to be the middle of a well, helpless at the end of the rope. The cold air blew up from below and struck chill, because he was sweating. It was with fear.

It was the kind of fear which seldom takes you in everyday life. It comes in dreams, in those nightmares when desperate things happen and you are the last living creature in a world that is breaking up and the fragments falling into bottomless chaos. Fear like that is something solid. It is made of steel, and has a razor edge. At the same time, it is vast and vague, shapeless as fog, and it smothers you with its horror. It is shameful, too: it breaks your pride and makes you crave to hide yourself away from your fellow men like a leper.

John put out his foot once more to try to stop himself from spinning round, but still he could not touch the wall. He was so giddy that he was tempted to close his eyes, but he told himself that to do so would be to surrender to something. He must keep on the alert, not only for possible dangers, but because in a situation like this he must not miss a single moment, or lose one fraction of the evidence contributing to the adventure.

He made another effort to control his spinning body, and to prevent himself from tugging at the rope. He told himself that it would be as unpleasant to go up as to go down, and that the bottom could only be a few yards below him. He found that by trying to control his breathing, slowly drawing in air until his lungs were full, he began to get some self-command. He took several of these deep breaths, and to his surprise, found that the whole of his body felt more firm and powerful. His fears, also, lost their grip, and he awaited what might happen next, awaited it with a growing calmness that astonished him. Astonishment itself added to his courage.

He needed that courage, for a moment later he realized that he was no longer going down. Not only had he been spinning round on the rope, he had also been swinging, and this had evidently frightened the people at the top who were paying the rope out, hand over hand. He felt his body grow heavier, and the rope began to cut him round the waist. He gripped the cord above him, eased his weight, threw back his head and looked up. The light from Alan's lamp dazzled him and he could see nothing except that distant star. But how far distant was it! 'Why have you stopped?' he shouted. The voice was not his own; it sounded more like a mouse squeaking in a trap; thin, terrified. He was ashamed to call a second time.

It was George who replied, and once again John recognized something uncommonly pleasant about his next-door neighbour. The gruff voice was hardly louder than a whisper, as though George had leaned over the edge of the pot-hole to speak confidentially, beyond the hearing of the other boys.

'It's all right,' he said, 'only a few feet more. Light a candle when you get there and test the air.' The gruffness of the voice was lost in the depths, and John could only hear what remained; something most friendly and reassuring.

'I'm spinning round,' he called back. 'Feeling a bit giddy.'

Before he could look down again, the rope had swung inward to within a few inches of the wall of the pot-hole. Instantly, he put out his foot to prevent a crash, and was partly successful. The effort flung him round, however, and the long torch tied to his waist caught against the rock and was torn away. The light went out and he heard the crash below him.

When a light goes out in a room, or under the open heaven of night, something remains, something recognizable, no matter how dimly it may shape itself in what we call the darkness swallowing that light. But to a man in the bowels of the earth where no star-shine can penetrate, where not even a glow-worm can exist, where nothing can be touched with the finger tips and known to be the shape of a chair, a table, a wall or a haystack; that indeed is a different sort of darkness. It is darkness total and absolute. It is darkness that springs instantly and from every side, like a horde of tigers, but tigers with blind eyes. It is darkness that comes down upon the brain, stops the breath in our bodies, and freezes our blood with terror.

This was the darkness that fell upon John Walters and closed round him as he swung in space at an unknown depth near the bottom of that underground shaft. This time fear gripped him and held firm. At first he could not think. He hung there, and hours might have passed, hours of nothingness. He was still easing the weight from his waist by gripping the rope above his head. He was conscious of a sharp pain down one thigh where he had grazed against the rock at the moment when his torch was torn from his side. He was almost grateful for that pain; it made him sure he was still a living, breathing person, still John Walters hanging on a rope with friends above him and the hope of finding a foot-hold somewhere below. There was no other indication of his identity except that pain. He dared to draw one hand from the rope above and to feel carefully with it over his face. He touched his cheeks and forehead and they were like touching a fish wet from the river. He rubbed his knuckles into his right eye and blinked. It was impossible to know whether his eyes were open or shut, for the closing or raising of an eyelid meant nothing in that utter darkness.

'Torch!' he shouted, and he was alive enough to know that the shout was really a scream. 'Torch!' he cried again, and he thought his voice was drowning. But someone heard him, and instantly the beam of light came reaching, searching like the knife of a surgeon groping its way skilfully. He heard Alan Hobbs say something, and it sounded as though Alan, too, had caught sight of the figure of fear. This did not comfort the boy at the end of the rope, and he longed to hear once again the gruff, almost grumpy tone of George Reynolds.

Meanwhile the movement of the rope had begun. It had begun a little too freely, and he appeared to be hurtling

He let himself down over the edge

down between the walls of the shaft towards an uncomfortable crash at the bottom. A voice above cried 'Steady', and he felt himself slowing up. Once more he thanked George, although after all it may have been Alan who had directed the movement. But it did not occur to John to think so.

He could see dimly now, though even the powerful beam from the electric lamp was thinned away against the moisture-blackened sides of the pot-hole, broken up by knobs and hollows, dull surfaces and patches of vegetable matter, thick and sullen, surfaces where darkness breeds and multiplies.

The pull of the rope on his waist was becoming unbearable and he was forced to ease his weight once more. Then suddenly, it was all over. He had touched bottom.

He was sitting crumpled up, his whole body shaking like a jelly. It was something to be on firm ground, and his mind snapped back into control. He groped for his inside pocket and found the little pencil torch which his uncle had given him to keep in reserve. By the light of this he peered about him, not daring to move in case he should be perched on some perilous point from which he might tumble to disaster. For that moment, however, he was safe enough. He found himself sitting on an even floor of rock which made the base of the great cone-shaped cavern, due to the sudden broadening out of the sides of the shaft from about twenty-five feet above him. The cone, however, was cut in half by a great fissure. From one side of the cleft to the other flowed the river whose babbling voice the boys had heard from so far above.

The river in its bed was so regular that it might have been a canal shaped by man. It was about twelve feet wide. He could not guess its depth. It flowed across his field of vision in deep silence, smooth and firm as the wet trunk of a beech tree, or the muscular limb of a Negro.

The sound of living water must come from somewhere beyond the floor of the cone. It meant that the stream went on, tracing its way through further hollows in the underworld; hollows, therefore, which could probably be explored by man – or boy. He gave the whole of his attention to this sound, and by thus selecting it, his ear magnified it and gave it a meaning. It called to him from the right-hand exit of the cone, and he knew that somewhere in that further darkness a waterfall dropped to yet deeper floors and distances.

He left that for the moment. He had still to locate himself, to make sure of his safety, to signal to the boys above, and to take the next step towards bringing little Lightning down the shaft. Doubt seized him, and he asked himself if it was right to let another human being suffer what he had gone through during the last quarter of an hour, or whatever time had elapsed since he left the others at the top. Before he could resolve this doubt, he was hailed by the boy whose fate he was considering.

'Hurry up, John,' piped the treble voice of Lightning, and this time it sounded more shrill and childlike than ever. 'What are you waiting for?' cried that eager piccolo. 'Can't you tug on the rope?'

John realized that he was still squatting where he had alighted, and that the rope was fastened round his waist. He loosened the knot, eased himself and drew the rope off his head. Still he held it above him in his hand, curiously unwilling to leave go of the lifeline. But there was no reason to hold it, and without further hesitation he gave two steady tugs, paused and repeated the signal. The response was instant. The rope leapt away into the semi-darkness above, writhing like a snake round the beam of light from the lamp. He stared at it fascinated until it disappeared. Then he knew that he was alone in this strange and utterly unknown place, cut off from mankind and the living earth. Not quite cut off, however, for once again the voice of the unseen waterfall clamoured for his attention. It was more than one voice, it was a multitude, whose cries blended into a music urging the listener crouched on the rock, urging and entreating him not to give way to fear, not to be baffled, not to believe that he was buried alive at the bottom of a well from which there was no means of escape.

By the aid of his tiny lamp, he looked about him for more immediate information. The rock floor on which he was sitting was so smooth and regular that, with the corresponding half on the other side of the stream, it might have been levelled by the hand of man. Both sides were clear of loose rubble, and this tidiness made one small object all the more noticeable. It squatted on the water's edge on the other side of the stream, and when John directed his torch light on it, a sulky ruby glittered near its top. He studied it more closely and then realized that the ruby eye was studying him too. The boy on one side of the river, and the toad on the other, breathed hard. John could see the loose bag below the toad's jaw rising and falling. The steady eye shone without blinking.

Several moments passed, for the boy was too startled to do anything. The spell was broken by the toad, who suddenly gave a gesture of disgust, slewed his loose body round, and flopped off towards the back away from the water, gradually melting into the darkness and shapelessness of the rocky angle where the sloping wall met the floor.

Assured at least of one companion, John forgot his solitude and began cheerfully to occupy his waiting moments by exploring farther with the small means at his command. He tried to test the depth of the stream, but the feeble ray of his torch could not penetrate the thick mass of water which flowed so smoothly. He tested the part where the stream entered and where it left. Both defeated his scrutiny. The entrance and the exit were shaped alike, the stream being surmounted by two arches like the wishbone of a chicken. Indeed, the likeness of the two, and the general symmetry of the cone with its level floor and the stream bisecting it, reminded John of one of the diagrams in his geometry book. The only thing out of place had been the toad. He forgot to add himself, the intruder; perhaps because he was too much occupied.

After the departure of the toad, however, John began to realize again that he was waiting there for Lightning to join him. He was still sitting directly beneath the pot-hole and had only to look up to see what might be towards. At

John forgot his solitude and began cheerfully to occupy his waiting moments by exploring farther

first nothing happened; then he heard a murmur of voices, and this was followed by the feeble flashing of a torch light as though some inquiry were being made as to his welfare. He put his hands to his mouth to form a trumpet, threw back his head and shouted, 'I'm all right. Is Lightning coming?'

The result was extraordinary. The cold air flowing up the well seized his words and twirled them like a little wisp of smoke up a draughty chimney. It snatched them out of his mouth and they were gone almost before they were fully formed on his lips. The whispering multitude of the waters ignored his efforts, but he was inclined to think that a note of mockery had crept into that perpetual murmuring.

The boys above, however, must have heard something, for the lamp flashed three times, paused, then flashed three times again. He remembered that he had said that three tugs on the rope was to mean that he wanted to be pulled up, and he now guessed that George had used this signal to tell him that Lightning was on his way down. He assumed that it was George because he had seen him write down the instructions while Alan was busy giving orders.

A few moments later, he saw a shadow come in front of the feeble star of light from the shaft top. It slowly grew larger, and he realized that it was the body of Harold Soames. As it grew nearer he could see that it was spinning round, and he longed to put up his arms to steady the little fellow. But the most friendly arm in the world cannot reach up fifty or sixty feet to help a neighbour in trouble, and John had to wait patiently, with his heart in his mouth, while Lightning drew nearer and nearer, a silent bundle empty of human form, but, alas, not of human feeling, as John knew from his own recent and unpleasant experience.

As the distance shrank, the real nature of the bundle on the end of the rope began to show itself. John shouted up to him and the plucky little chap answered cheerfully.

The descent was now slower, for whoever was directing operations at the top had the sense to foresee the danger of hitting the buffers at the terminus. Movement ceased, as it had done with John, and there was much inquiry from the top, and conflict of voices speculating on the distance reached by the second explorer. John cupped his hands again and shouted up the shaft, one word at a time: 'Ten . . . more . . . feet . . .'

Somebody replied.

It was curious how sounds refused to come down the shaft. Inch by inch, Lightning began to move again, and

John could see him kicking out with his legs, feeling for firm ground.

'Keep still,' he shouted, 'or you will kick me in the face. I'm going to catch you.' The kicking ceased, and John jumped up, flung his arms round Lightning and eased him gently to the ground, so gently that he arrived on his feet, much to his own amazement.

John was surprised at his own next movement. He found himself still with arms round Lightning, hugging him close in a kind of ecstasy of thankfulness, either at the boy's safe arrival, or his own relief from that grim state of absolute solitude.

Nobody could remain still, however, within a yard of Lightning. He now wriggled like an eel, so eager was he to find out for himself what things were like at the bottom of the shaft. He appeared to need no time to recover from possible giddiness. His compass was in his hand and he was studying it by the light of his torch.

'Be quiet,' he said, dodging away from John, who was looking over his shoulder, trying to peer at the compass. 'What a beauty! Look how it works.' His whole attention was fixed upon the little instrument in his hand. The rest of the world didn't matter, and he seemed quite unimpressed by the fact that a few moments ago he had dropped about eighty feet on the end of a rope towards unknown dangers in the depths of the earth.

'Keep still,' he muttered, speaking as much to himself as to his companion.

His bright eager eyes followed the movement of the magnetic needle as it flickered and floated and gradually came to rest. 'We're on the north bank,' he said, and his voice was awe-stricken as though he had made one of the great discoveries in human history. 'That's the south side over there,' and he pointed with his arm and one finger extended, while he still stared with his face close to the dial of the compass.

This information excited John.

'That's what I thought,' he said. 'It means the river's flowing westward, and that we came in at the back of the big cave. This stream must come round from behind us. I wonder if it flows through and meets it again? If so, we may be able to follow it and get back to the floor of the big cave.'

He pondered for a few moments. 'But this level is surely deeper than the floor of the cave.'

Having satisfied themselves about the direction of the flow of the river, the boys now began to consider their position, and what they should do next. Lightning had brought the ball of twine with him and also a hammer and chisel. 'George told me to,' he said. They decided that not much purpose would be served by exploring *up*stream. The thing was to try to connect up this chamber with the greater one above, and if possible to reunite the party. They must search *down*-river.

They set about telling the others what they were going to do. Both cursed themselves for not having learned Morse, and promised to master the code before next holidays. John took out his pad, wrote down the message and tied it to the loop of the rope, gave it two tugs and then the second two tugs. He also shouted up the shaft and heard a cry in response. He then expected to see the rope drawn up. Indeed, it began the ascent, but it had hardly left the ground when he heard another cry from the top of the shaft, this time a cry of alarm. A moment later, there was a whizzing noise, the rope leapt down and in an instant the whole length of it flopped in a heap at their feet. A silence followed, then an outburst of voices, all too distant to be distinguished or understood. John thought he heard someone crying, but that may have been his fancy. One thing was certain, there lay the rope at their feet, and what had been their lifeline was now a useless mass. They were cut off from the people at the top. It was probable, indeed, that they were cut off altogether from human life. John stared at Lightning and Lightning stared at John across the pile of rope. The voices above had ceased. They heard the chuckling of water. Little Soames put his compass into his trouser pocket.

'We're trapped,' he said, and there was almost a note of triumph in his voice.

'Yes, we're trapped,' echoed John, but he was not triumphant. His mind was working forward, inquiring eagerly, desperately, if there was a way along the bed of the stream.

'What do we do now?' asked Lightning.

John looked at him, and felt a curious lump in his throat. He could not reply, so he shook his head in such a way that his companion could interpret this sign as he liked.

'Come on, then,' said Lightning, 'let's find a way out.'

CHAPTER 9

THE VOICE OF AUTHORITY

IT was Meaty Sanders who had broken down and cried like a child. Everybody was so surprised that the hot words blew away like steam off a stove. Meaty, with his huge body as strong as that of a blacksmith, his total lack of fear, and his appetite as big as that of three fully grown men, had always been respected by other boys. People took care not to fall foul of him. Certainly it was not difficult, because Meaty was a friendly person and would not have hurt a wasp, still less a fly. Had the other boys been wise enough, or had the circumstances been more calm, Meaty's sudden outcry and flood of tears might almost have been expected. They were due to his extreme good nature.

Nobody was quite sure how the trouble began. George and Meaty were standing close to the wall paying out the rope with scientific care, each crossing an arm alternately over that of the other so that the rope was never allowed to slip away from a continuous grasp. To do this, they stood side by side with a foot well advanced and their bodies thrown back to keep a steady balance. Meaty knew all about these things because his brother was first mate of a merchant ship, trading round the coast from Bristol. How it was that George fell into the right position and worked, as it were, hand in glove, or rather rope in hand, with Meaty, must remain unexplained, for he had never learned much about boats from any member of his family. One look at the boat-house at the river-end of his garden would show that. Dumb George Reynolds, shy and retiring, managed to surprise people at unexpected moments. The curious thing was that people forgot to be surprised an instant after the event. They remembered what he had done and quietly readjusted the picture of him in their minds. The thin strong rope moved steadily down the pathway formed by the rope ladder. All went well, as smoothly as though it were winding off a winch. Lightning stood in front of the other two throwing the light of his torch along the rope and towards the shaft. At the head of it knelt Alan Hobbs who was peering over the edge with one arm stretched down holding the big lamp with its focused beam concentrated on the figure of John Walters as it grew smaller and smaller below. The shadow of Alan, cast by Lightning's torch, was thrown on the opposite wall. It was the size and shape of a small elephant, and every time that Alan moved, the elephant appeared to be struggling up from its knees.

Paying out of the rope went on steadily until Alan shouted that John was swinging dangerously and that they ought to stop. He got up from his knees, thus plunging the shaft into darkness.

'I say,' said George, 'you mustn't switch off your lamp. He must need that light badly down there.'

'He's got his own torch, hasn't he?' said Alan snappily.

'Even if he has,' broke in Meaty, 'we can't leave him swinging in space. It's no joke down there, I bet.'

This criticism from two sides upset Alan.

'Someone's got to run the thing,' he said, angrily, 'it's a responsible job, especially now he's nearing the bottom.'

He had, however, returned to the edge of the shaft and switched on his lamp again; but that shadow on the opposite wall had the appearance of a very peevish elephant. Work went on in silence, and even Lightning was quiet.

'His torch has gone out,' said Alan, suddenly. 'What's happened? I can't see. Wait a minute. Now I've got him. Lower slowly now. Gently; slower still. I believe he's near the bottom – '

'I know he's on the bottom,' groaned George. 'The weight's gone.'

'Good work,' said Meaty, 'I was getting hot round the

collar. Jobs like that make me feel I've been starved for a week. Are you hungry, too, George?'

Alan's delayed temper now broke. He got up from his knees and with his lamp turned upward to the ceiling of the chamber and throwing a general radiance on them all, he advanced on the two boys, who still stood with the rope in their hands. He pushed past Lightning.

'Look here, you two! I couldn't say anything while you'd got John hanging on the rope, but now I'm telling you what I think. I gave you an instruction at a critical moment and you questioned it. That's not the way things are run, and if it happens again there's going to be trouble.'

Meaty stared at him in pained surprise. George was affected differently. He looked guilty, turned his head to the right and to the left as though looking for a place to hide.

Lightning was the only one left unmoved. That was because he was too quick in all he did; he had no time to bother with what people said or thought. Maybe even he didn't hear them, or was quite incapable of being conscious of criticism.

There they all stood for some moments, an uneasy gathering, and something more ugly might have cropped up had not Meaty's right hand suddenly twitched forward. John was signalling from below.

The two pulls on the rope were repeated.

'Haul up,' said George, and he and Meaty began carefully to pull in the rope. By the time the loop had reached the surface, Alan appeared to have recovered his temper, and no more was said. He did not notice that George glanced secretly at him from time to time, wondering about something.

The next problem was how to prevent Lightning from leaping down the shaft before the rope could be adjusted round his waist.

'Come along! Hurry up,' he cried several times, bobbing

up and down on his toes, and flashing his torch on and off for no purpose whatever.

'Keep still, you flea,' said Meaty, putting a massive hand on the top of his head. 'How do you think we can fix up the rope while you dance about?'

They managed to sober him, and to din into his mind a few words of advice.

'And look here,' said Alan to the urchin sitting with his feet over the edge, while the other two boys had returned to their stations behind the pegs and the coil of rope, 'when you're down there, remember that John is in charge. He acts on my authority.'

This command silenced everybody. The four boys stood looking at each other for some moments. From the bottom of the well there rose again the music of the river like distant voices, and then they heard a thin and hollow cry from John asking if Lightning was coming. This broke the spell. Alan returned to the edge and flashed the lamp three times and again three times. Meanwhile, Meaty gathered in the rope at his feet at the back of the cave and gave it two passes round the pegs.

Easing Lightning over the edge was a simple matter, for the boys were now experienced, and knew how the rope would behave. They paid it out more quickly, believing that a rapid descent might prevent the spinning motion which had so alarmed them when John was going down. This theory proved to be right and Lightning dropped from sight like a plummet, and it seemed only a matter of seconds after his weight had eased from the rope that the signal to haul up came. Indeed, they were not prepared for it so soon. Alan had left the edge and rejoined the two by the pegs. When the repeated double tug came, it startled him because he was standing against the rope, which twitched against his ankle. He was evidently excited or nervous about something, because he jumped away with an exclamation, and in doing so kicked against one of the chisels, stumbled, and shook it out of its hold in the floor. The rope immediately leapt with its tension back on the other chisel, but by this time, Meaty had been easing the knot in order to start recoiling. The end of the rope leapt from his hands and fell to the ground half-way towards the edge of the pit. He was after it instantly, but in doing so had to push Alan aside. The leader had not seen what had happened, and once again his temper took command.

He jumped round and saw Meaty already hauling on the rope. He was full of suspicion. He believed that the push was intentional, and was aimed, not so much at him, as at his leadership. And about this he was already uneasy. He had to do something to reassert his authority.

'Stop,' he cried, 'I didn't tell you to do that.' He stepped forward and laid a hand on the rope.

Meaty Sanders was a massive boy of unknown strength, but his wits did not work very fast. He was startled, and his hands dropped from the rope in order, if necessary, to defend himself against this unexpected attack from a boy with whom he had thought himself on good terms, and whose leadership he had no mind to dispute. At the same moment, an uneasy feeling must have struck Alan, for he, too, let go of the rope, and both boys saw it strike the ground, leap up and over the edge of the shaft.

The effect was paralysing. All three knew what this meant. It meant more than their poor wits could take in before the shock had subsided. It was then that Meaty Sanders broke down and cried like a child.

This did not last long, however, for George put out a hand, took him by the arm and drew him back to the wall of the cave. He said nothing but just stood there, beside Meaty with a large bony hand clasping his arm. The touch calmed and startled the giant, who blew his nose and muttered 'Sorry'. After which the incident was closed.

Something had to be done, and done quickly. It was George who did it.

Both boys saw it leap up and over the edge of the shaft

'Flash your lamp to them,' he said to Alan, who still stood on the spot where he had attacked Meaty. 'They'll be feeling blue.'

Then he turned to Meaty. 'You stay with him, Meaty,' he said, 'while I see if there is a way down farther along the platform. None of us looked there, after all. We came straight through this tunnel. Try to let them know what I am doing. You could write a message, wrap it round a stone and drop it over.'

There was a touch of drama in George's imagination, an odd thing in such a slow, dumb sort of a fish. He must have known that it was possible to shout down the shaft, because Lightning had already done so to tell John that he was coming down.

Before either of the boys could point this out, however, George had stepped back through the ten-foot passage and was gone.

Meaty was left with Alan, who said nothing. He evidently was sulking, but now that George had disappeared, he felt more able to deal with the slow-witted Meaty.

'That was a fool's trick,' he said, without looking round. Perhaps he did not want to show his face. 'See where you've landed us now. That comes of not obeying instructions.'

Poor Meaty said nothing, because he was beginning to blame himself again, if indeed he was thinking of himself at all. What really worried him was the state of the two boys at the bottom of the shaft. He felt responsible for little Lightning. His silence encouraged Alan.

'Who told you to start hauling the rope in?' he asked. 'I know I didn't.' He was now bold enough to look round once more. He even turned the beam of his lamp on to the boy whom he was accusing of being the guilty party. He did not mind leaving the two unfortunate comrades below for a few moments of bewildering darkness. 'Yes,' he said, now glaring at Meaty like an angry colonel, 'I warned you all just now what would happen if everybody tried to take the lead.'

By this time, Meaty was reduced to shame, and ready to be convinced that he was solely the cause of the accident.

'Sorry, Alan,' he said, 'I want to put it right,' casting his huge body about, and clasping his hands together in his anxiety and remorse.

CHAPTER 10

MAN ALONE

WHEN George left the ten-foot passage and re-entered the big cave, he stood still for a few moments to accustom his eyes to the dim yellow light of his dark-lantern. He knew that it was urgent to find a way to rescue John and Lightning, but he deliberately held himself back while he thought things out.

There was not much thinking to do, however, for the only unexplored area was the farther reach of the platform which the boys had neglected. He therefore turned left and walked along close to the wall, aware that the outer edge of the platform was narrowing as he proceeded.

He could feel his heart thumping, and he knew that the situation was likely to be desperate if he should find that the platform came to an end without offering a passage to the floor of the cave or some unknown outlet beyond.

The light of his lamp was steady but so poor that he dared not hurry for fear of stumbling. As he groped along, and the platform began to narrow down to a mere ledge again, he was also in danger of stepping over the edge. To add to the danger, the ledge now began to ascend steeply, and its surface became shaley and treacherous with loose rubbish.

Then it suddenly turned a corner into a bay, hitherto unseen, near the farther reaches of the cave. The rock wall threw out a buttress at this angle and cut the path in two.

George stopped. The throbbing had now risen to his throat and he could feel his hands sweating. He tried turning the lamp up a little so that he might throw its beam, if so feeble a light could be called a beam, over the protruding rock to see where the ledge was resumed. But the lamp only smoked and changed its yellow light to a sulky blood-red glow that left him practically in darkness. His hand shook as he turned the wick down again, with the result that he almost put the flame out. But he managed to save it, and he drew a deep breath while he slapped the outside of his pocket to reassure himself that his matches were still there.

He climbed up and held out his lamp at arm's length, to make sure the path continued without a gap between it and the farther side of the rock that stood in his way. All looked solid enough and he had now only to bestride the rock and strike the ledge on the other side, where it carried on at a level some three or four feet higher. The action was like climbing over a gigantic vaulting-horse, a simple matter in a well-lit gymnasium, but more complicated for a boy loaded with a rope, a stick, a dark-lantern, a haversack and a heavy heart. The heavy heart, however, now proved to be George's helper, for he was driven on by an increasing anxiety about his friends at the bottom of the pot-hole. Otherwise, he might well have hesitated and even turned back before this present obstacle, which seemed to grow bigger as he looked at it; or tried to look at it, for the darkness was now terrifying. He could hear the regular drip, drip of the drops of water, falling from the roof into the pool below, and also the distant music of the river by whose deep, flowing waters his friends were now seated.

Suddenly it occurred to him that it was odd that he should still be hearing the voice of the river. It was indeed as loud as when he had heard it from the head of the pot-hole. But between him and that spot there now stretched a quarter of the circumference of the great cave and the ten-foot thickness of rock between the cave and that second chamber.

He listened intently, leaning forward with his head half

across the rock wall. He withdrew, listened again, compared the sounds from the two positions. There was no doubt about it; with his head craning forward over the path beyond the obstacle he could hear the sound of the river more distinctly. There must be a way out!

This faint promise gave him heart. No longer allowing himself to hesitate, he reached over and lodged his lantern in a little niche on the other side. This left him in darkness under the shadow of the great rock, but he had memorized his next foothold and he now groped with his left foot and both arms, hoisted himself up, and a minute later was safely on the other side. It had been a long minute! He paused for breath, reached up for his lantern and grasped it. He had, however, misjudged his distance and instead of taking it by the handle, he seized the lantern itself. The pain of the burn was so unexpected that his whole arm jerked back, his knuckles crashed against the rock wall, and the shock made him stumble.

The pain did not cease. Indeed, it grew more and more fiery, for he had seized the lantern firmly, and now the whole palm of his hand, as well as his finger tips, was pulsing and throbbing. There he stood, still in danger of falling, blinded by agony, and unable to see more than a yard or two even had his vision not been ruined by pain. But still he could hear that sound of promise, the faint lip, lip of water, somewhere in the region still unexplored round the large bay which, in relation to the rest of the cave, was like a transept of a cathedral between the nave and the chancel.

George half turned, and looked backward at the buttress which he had just crossed. From this side, although lower, it looked more forbidding than ever. He tried to stare down into the great space below; but that was both useless and frightening. The ledge about three feet wide lay between him and extinction, a ledge whose surface was littered with slippery pieces of shale. He thanked heaven for the thinness of the soles of his old gym. shoes, for through them he could feel the loose surface and knew that with care he could pick his way safely.

Standing with his back to the wall, he groped for his handkerchief and bound it round his burnt hand. The touch of the cotton on his skin sharpened the pain for a moment, but he took no heed of this for he had become obstinate, and nothing should prevent him from making his way onwards. This time, he took up his lantern with care and began to walk round the curve of the ledge into the interior of the bay.

As so often happens when one turns a corner, the new scene began to loom larger than the one left behind. George was astonished to find himself penetrating farther and farther inwards at right angles to the main body of the cavern. The darkness here seemed to be deeper, but that may have been due to an increasing chill in the air. He could now hear more clearly the murmur of water, and this led him to speculate about his position in relation to the two boys at the bottom of the pot-hole, and the two at the top of it beyond the tunnel leading out of the big cave. He told himself that the river was obviously much lower than the floor of the cave, because he and Meaty had paid out practically the whole hundred-foot rope when lowering the two boys. Therefore, if the water which he could hear was the same river flowing openly at the bottom of this transept cavern, then the floor below him must have dropped some forty feet from the floor of the main cave. This, together with the passage of constantly flowing water, might account for the change in the temperature which he could feel as much in his mind as on his skin. A dismal thought struck him, however; if his theory was right, then the odds were heavier against his being able to get down to water level so that he could begin to look for a break through to John and young Lightning.

The fear of that, and the increasing gloom and remoteness

of this new phase of the adventure, so weighed upon his spirits that he stopped in dismay.

The last shuffle of his feet sent an echo fluttering round the walls of the unknown extension of the underground world. Partly to keep up his courage, and partly to test by ear and guesswork the dimensions of the new cave, he smote the wall of the rock with his stick, and gave all his attention to the journey made by the echo of that sharp slap. There was a long pause before the first mock sound jeered back at him, to be followed instantly by a babble of decreasing imitations, dying away in a spiral of sound down towards the unseen floor. His thoughtful mind gravely and deliberately pondered on that interval between the slap of the stick on the wall and the first echo. He was awe-stricken; so much so, that he muttered aloud, 'My word, it must be wider than the other.'

Knowing that nothing further could be done by taking thought without fresh evidence, he set off again along the ledge round what promised to be the great curve of the bay. When he reached the back of it, however, he found that the ledge came to an abrupt end, proving itself to be the protruding lip of a gigantic flaw in the wall of the cave. This flaw now struck inward and cut the wall in two. He found that the ledge turned into this fissure, and he walked along it through the split in the rock with the great walls soaring up on each side of him at little more than an arm's length.

The passage was about thirty feet long. It opened on yet another cave which, to his surprise, offered a dim light. He now heard the voice of the river even more loudly than when it came to him at the top of the pot-hole. The music, indeed, was now a merry tumult like that of a crowd of children released from school.

He was immediately encouraged by the sound of the river. He needed this help, for that walk through the passage between the walls of rock had made him shudder.

But now, the sense of freedom gave him hope. Here, too, was a new turn to the adventure, one which must surely help him to find a way to get to John and Lightning.

The light, also, what did that mean? He closed the shutter of his dark-lantern so that he should offer no rivalry to this new source of light. Everything was dim, but even so, shapes and masses could be distinguished, and that was a different state of affairs from those he had left behind in the great cave and the great bay. He began to see more clearly and found that the ledge branched to right and left, the former branch dwindling away until it disappeared into the rock face. He ventured upon it, however, creeping cautiously until there was no further foothold. From here he could view the depths below. An extraordinary spectacle greeted his eyes. There in the farthest right-hand corner of the cave he saw what appeared to be a lamp in the waters of the river. It threw green and blue beams through the water and broke into all the colours of the rainbow as the water played upon it, wave over wave, like a cat's paws over a captive mouse. The paws of the river, however, were of crystal and the light shone through them even as they patted at it.

As he watched this pretty game between light and water, he traced the source of it. It was a hole close to the bed of the stream. Round this hole, the dammed-up river was heaving and struggling like a crowd pushing through a doorway. Then he suddenly realized that this *was* a doorway. It was a doorway into the outer world, the world of sunshine and liberty and comparative safety. He stared at it, fascinated, his mind hungry with excitement. It seemed to be mocking him, the circumference of the hole changing shape and pulsing like a blood-filled heart. The grey light which made objects in the cavern faintly discernible, was just the outer fringe from that flexible mass of cold fire beating in the bed of the river.

After the first impulse of excitement, it was the greyness

of the diffused light which took command of his spirits and sobered him. He realized that he was no nearer his goal and that he must get busy. To this end, he now began to explore the left-hand branch of the ledge, first turning on the beam of his dark-lantern which competed fairly successfully with the filtered light from the outside world.

He was soon brought to a standstill, for the path was broken by a sharp drop of some fifteen feet to another ledge which sloped away rapidly to the interior of the cave, at present lost in darkness and beyond the reach of the feeble beam from his lantern.

George stood at the top of this miniature precipice and calculated the angle of the slope of the ledge below. He decided that with care he could scramble down it, for it appeared to be wider than the one he was standing on. He next looked about for a means of getting down to this lower ledge. Fortunately, there was a stump of round rock that formed a sort of buffer-end to the abrupt termination of the upper ledge. This could be used as a capstan round which a rope could be thrown for a man to lower himself down those fifteen feet. That was what the last man of the party would have to do.

This decision made, he turned back to fetch Alan and Meaty. It was not a pleasant job because it meant losing time. There was another reason too why it was unpleasant. He had to climb back over that buttress of rock where the ledge turned at right angles in the main cave. The thought of this made him go cold, and the larger fear drove out the smaller one, which he might have felt as he returned along that narrow passage of thirty feet between those appalling walls of rock which threatened to close together as he crept between them like an insect.

His hands were again clammy with sweat, and he could feel his burnt palm throbbing violently. It was impossible to do anything about this until he got back to the head of the pot-hole, where John had dumped the first-aid kit.

He was in darkness again, darkness that by comparison with the glimmer of light from the farther cave, now seemed absolute. It made him breathless. He toiled on, however, retracing his steps one by one along the ledge until he reached the dreaded obstacle. He had now to find a preliminary foothold on this side, by which to mount. While peering about with his lantern close to the flank of the buttress, which he could have sworn had grown in bulk during his few minutes' absence, he found himself wondering what Alan would make of this.

Once again a spasm of fear shook him. He realized that he was beginning to doubt his confidence in Alan's leadership. John, the boy he would have turned to, was a prisoner at the bottom of that pot-hole, and in danger of his life. George was thinking this over while he swung himself up over the back of this terrifying vaulting-horse. This time, he kept his lantern in his hand, and sat astride the top of the rock still thinking things out. He was so lost in thought, indeed, that it did not occur to him to look round over the flanks of this grim steed. He did not see, therefore, that they sloped away into space and that a jerk in the saddle would throw him down to destruction.

Once over the obstacle, he hurried back to Alan and Meaty. He found them lying on their stomachs, peering over the edge of the pot-hole which they were trying to illuminate with the light from the lamp and Meaty's torch. They were so intent on this that they ignored the return of their companion. Meaty spoke to him without looking up: 'They've gone!' he wheezed, breathless with the effort of supporting his bulk in a horizontal position.

'Shut up,' said Alan. 'We shan't hear them if you talk.'

He still sounded frightened. It may have been that he was wondering what the others were thinking about him. He knew that they had seen him stumble over that chisel, a clumsy action which had been the cause of the lifeline disappearing. The return of George made him uneasy. It might be a simple matter to switch the blame on to Meaty Sanders. He was simple enough to take it, and Alan had gambled on that certainty. George was an unknown quantity, however; a boy who said little, and concealed his thoughts. That was why Alan now lay face downward, deliberately giving his attention to problems at the bottom of the shaft. 'We've got to get these fellows up,' he said, with an air of heavy responsibility.

'But where are they?' asked George. 'Have they given you a message?'

'Yes, they've signalled that they intend to explore downstream, to try and find where it breaks through.'

This news made George spring to life again, and once more his manner and conduct surprised his fellow explorers.

'Good,' he grunted, with an emphasis that brought both boys to their knees. 'That's exactly what I wanted them to do. I believe I've found a way down to meet them.' He paused, frowned, then added with an energy that brought Alan and Meaty up from their knees: 'We've *got* to get through to them, there's no other way to save them.'

Alan felt himself being brushed aside.

'Yes,' he began, 'and I think – '

'We've no time for argument,' said George. He spoke quietly, but there was a quality in his voice which silenced Alan. 'I've found that the path along the ledge breaks into another cave through which the river is flowing. There's a faint trace of daylight in it, which means that we may be able to follow the river out. The thing now is to get down to the stream and find where it breaks from the inner cave where John and Lightning are trapped.' He returned to his usual sombre and hesitant manner: 'Yes, that's what we've got to do: we've got to find them.'

He patted his pockets as though feeling for something. He found his small drawing-block, half drew it from his pocket and looked at it longingly, as though wishing to confide something to it. Then he thrust it down with a vigorous hand and started off, calling as he went: 'Come along, we'd better hurry.'

Although he set the example, he did not forget to gather up as much of the clobber as he could carry. And still he had not done anything with the first-aid box towards bandaging his burnt hand.

CHAPTER II

DOWN RIVER

WHEN Lightning said: 'Let's find a way out,' he and John were squatting on their heels like two Red Indians before a camp fire. Their fire, however, consisted of one candle flame, which John had managed to kindle after wasting four matches, blown out by the draught running along the river. The boys had retreated to the shelter of a recess where wall and floor met. Within this cubby hole they were snug enough to regain courage and to hold a council of action. Lightning, excited by his own words, jumped up so abruptly that he gave his head a crack on the rock.

John heard the crunch, and was alarmed to see Lightning stagger. The wild imp was so eager, however, that he ignored, or pretended to ignore, this interruption of his enthusiasm. Rubbing his head ruefully and sucking in his breath in the effort to control the pain, he cried out: 'Come on, man, come on, don't waste time.'

While John was in the act of obeying this trumpet call, he saw a dark smudge spreading down Lightning's forehead. Next moment, the boy flicked his hand across his eye impatiently. The result was a widening of the smudge and a shining streak across his button-nose.

'Wait a bit,' said John, 'your head's bleeding.'

And so it was; bleeding freely, for the drops were now gathering on his eyebrows and blinding him.

'Stand still, you idiot,' commanded John. 'This comes of being in a hurry. We shall want all our strength, I expect, and we can't afford to lose blood.'

He was trying to speak severely, as a tonic to prevent Lightning from being frightened; for often the bravest of people are afraid of the sight of blood. But John need not have been anxious, for Lightning was not to be subdued.

'Ooh, that's nothing,' he cried, and his voice was more than ever like the top note from a piccolo. Maybe, it trembled a little, but nobody would have noticed that. He might even have continued to dance and prance and make other gestures of excitement had not John seized him by the shoulder and forced him to kneel down near the light of the candle.

'Let me look,' he said.

'Oh, don't be an ass,' cried Lightning, beginning to struggle.

This effort, however, made the wound in his head bleed more freely, and once again he was blinded. John knew how to handle him. 'Stop it, Lightning,' he said, quietly. 'You'll make us both in a frightful mess, and we've got a lot to do.'

His patient appeal quietened the excitable child, who now submitted and allowed his head to be examined.

'My word,' said John, 'lucky it's not up in your hair. You've broken the skin just at the top of your forehead. You must have been star-gazing when you hit the roof. Shows what a foolhardy idiot you are.'

Nothing could have pleased Lightning more than this accusation. The idea of being a dare-devil who leapt before he looked was one which he had been cultivating all his life in order to counteract the loving care of a doting mother and a multitude of sisters. John had struck the right note and this, together with his careful avoidance of any expression of kindness, brought Lightning to heel. John took him by the arm and led him across the floor to the edge of the stream. He put his fingers into the water, and found it icy cold.

'Yes,' he said, 'that ought to stop it.'

He made Lightning lie flat on his stomach with his head protruding over the water, and then he began to splash the water up from his cupped hand. The boy gasped and jerked his head back at the first impact of the water on his broken skin. The treatment quickly worked, and a few minutes later, John was able to relax his efforts. Blood began to coagulate over the wound.

'We want a bandage now,' he said, 'but I've left the first-aid kit at the top.'

Then an amusing thing happened, which John was able to see because at that moment, as he spoke, he was examining the wound by the light of his pocket torch. A slow blush rose over Lightning's pale, eager little face. He looked shyly at John and said, almost in a whisper, 'I believe one of my sisters once sewed a small flat first-aid tin into the lining of my coat.' He patted the side of his coat. John seized the garment and, sure enough, there was something solid there not to be got at through the pockets. He took out his pen-knife, ripped the lining and pulled out the little flat box, hardly larger than a puncture outfit. Within a few minutes, he had plastered up the broken head and the adventurers were in good condition for the next stage of their exploration. That was how they looked at it; neither wanted to suggest that it was a necessary effort to save their own lives.

Leaving Lightning by the water's edge, John went back for the candle and the coil of rope. As he stooped to pick up the rope, which they had coiled where it had fallen, he saw his torch whose fall had been broken by a patch of moss. By the light of the candle he examined it and found that the bulb had gone, but that there was no other damage. He quickly fitted his spare bulb and the torch sprang to life again. Thereupon, he blew out the candle, allowed it to get cold, and put it in his pocket against further emergencies. Shouting his good news to Lightning, he then rejoined him and they were about to make off downstream when he remembered that he had not told the party at the top of the pot-hole what they intended to do. Returning to what he believed to be the centre of the shaft, he threw back his head, hollowed his hands around his mouth, and let forth a yodelling cry. His own voice startled him. It sounded absurdly cheerful coming from a fellow in danger of his life.

'George!' he shouted; but then he corrected himself suddenly, and at the second call shouted, 'Are you there, Alan?' And somehow, the second call was not quite so hearty.

The reply was delayed. First, the beam of light came searching down the pot-hole, leaping across from wall to wall and throwing a dusty circle of gold on the floor around him. Then he heard a voice; but it was neither that of Alan nor George.

'Are you all right?' cried Meaty Sanders; but it sounded like a Meaty grown thin and ghostly.

'Yes,' he shouted back. It was simple enough to throw up one word to the watchers at the top, but as soon as he tried to pitch them a sentence, the string of words came tumbling down over him like a rope recoiling after being thrown into the air. So he began again, flinging up one word at a time.

'We . . . are . . . going . . . to . . . follow . . . the . . . river . . . to . . . find . . . a . . . way . . . out. . . . Can . . . you . . . work . . . with . . . us . . .?'

These words went up the shaft like stars from a rocket, and somehow Meaty managed to catch them.

'O.K.!' he shouted down, 'George . . . has . . . already . . . started . . . to . . . look . . . for . . . a . . . path . . . down. . . .'

John, gleeful because of this news, was about to rejoin Lightning, when he heard another call from above. It was Alan. 'You there,' said the voice of authority, 'don't forget you're under instructions.' It was said too rapidly, however, and the effect came down the shaft rather blurred, while the last word sounded rather like 'destruction', and this was not calculated to cheer up the two poor wretches at the bottom.

'What did he say?' asked Lightning, picking up the rope which John had laid beside him.

‘Something or other,’ replied John, dully, thinking of other matters. Both of them guessed what Alan had said, but were content to leave it without comment. Somebody had to be in authority after all, so why not let Alan prove that he could live up to it?

John relieved Lightning of the coil of rope and put it over his left shoulder like a bandolier.

‘Have we got everything?’ he asked. They had to make sure before they could answer this question, and again their start was delayed. They returned to the little cubby hole where they had been squatting and there found an extremely dirty handkerchief belonging to Lightning. They prodded and patted themselves, going over the imaginary list of their possessions: the rope, Lightning’s compass (John had still not revealed that he had one in reserve); each a candle and matches and a good torch with extra batteries, Lightning having also a spare bulb, a hammer and chisel; one small first-aid box, one bag of wrapped barley sugars supplied by John, two bars of chocolate.

Satisfied that nothing was left behind, and that the people upstairs knew of their plan, the two explorers moved off. They walked tandem-wise along the right bank of the stream, which continued as firm and smooth as the edge of a swimming bath. The wall of the shaft opened out where the stream approached it and introduced the boys to a tunnel whose base was almost filled by the water. The left-hand bank faded out and the water lapped that side of the tunnel. Fortunately, the bank on which the boys were walking carried on through the tunnel at least as far as they could see by the light of the leader’s torch. Lightning was in front because John felt responsible for him and believed that he could exert a more restraining hand from behind.

‘Not too fast, now,’ he said. ‘We don’t know what we’re in for yet.’

So they went, step by step, slowly forward, following the single light of the torch which rose and fell with the rhythm of Lightning's cat-like steps. Farther and farther into the tunnel it led them, like a will-o'-the-wisp. Neither of them looked back. Had he done so, he would have seen an eye watching them. The lumpy, dusty old toad had come out again from his hole and was squatting where he had squatted before, the breath thumping in his throat and the baleful fire of his ruby eye returning a last broken glint of light caught from the disappearing torch. The stream ran heedlessly by him, and still he sat there long after the light had disappeared and the explorers had followed it round a bend in the tunnel.

The boys had not gone many yards round that bend before the thing happened which they had been half anticipating. The path on the right-hand side of the stream also disappeared, ending in a little jetty that stuck out into the stream, then dropped below the water to a rift in the bed, thus forming the narrow and noisy waterfall which they had heard from the bottom of the pot-hole.

John and Lightning stood side by side on the little jetty, staring at the waterfall. John had put his arm round Lightning's shoulders because the foothold looked precarious. There was another reason, too; the picture before them was one which had to be shared. Both boys had switched on their torches, and the two lights played on the flowing water, moving uncertainly to and fro as though searching under the direction of the minds behind the hands that held the torches.

The beams were like two spirits hovering there, uncertain, awaiting instruction from some other authority. There was good reason to pause. For one thing, the boys were puzzled about the next step; for another, the beauty of the waterfall under the light of the torches was something that arrested even the impetuous Lightning. He stood beside John, his little snub nose sticking out and sniffing at the metallic smell of the underground stream.

The river stopped its music as it approached the fall, and

the little wavelets merged into two deep, smooth muscles of water that twisted inward before grappling with some tremendous task. Then, at the rim of the ridge, the tension broke, and the smooth silent mass poured over into a self-created gulf that beat and thundered and foamed into a pool six feet below. This pool, however, was far too small to contain the volume that rushed, moment by moment, from the stillness above. The great mass of seething water was, therefore, shot upward and forward across the pool and along the farther bed of the stream. The river thus appeared to be flowing upward, climbing and snarling with angry claws up the face of the rock bed along the farther reaches of the tunnel, whose walls thenceforward gleamed wet with the flung spray from the cauldron. No doubt all this would have been a drama even in darkness, but the light of the two torches changed it into a tempestuous fairyland, where rainbow clashed with rainbow like multi-coloured swords, and the silver bullets of the spray hurled like tracer shot in all directions.

At the farther end of the rim where the water poured over, a cluster of fungi was pinned to the rock wall. These flesh-coloured brackets attracted the boys' attention at once, and both flashed their torches on the sinister objects. From moment to moment, a drop of water, tossed from the cauldron below, alighted on the leathery surface of the fungi and was at once absorbed, leaving a thumb mark of stain which instantly followed the water drop into oblivion. Thus, the surface of these brackets was constantly in colour-motion, like the keyboard of a piano when the player's fingers are pressing down the ivories, making momentary shadows on the white surface. Added to that play of colour, the substance of the fungi trembled somewhat, as though shivering within its own stillness. All this gave it the appearance of being alive. The little brackets might have been half-formed human hands, born from the rock and trembling under the impulse of some remote fear.

How long Lightning and John had been watching these objects, they could not tell, so strong was the spell. They were recalled to reality, however, by the spray which had gathered on John's spectacles. The moment came when he could see nothing except a blur of broken light, and he had to take off his spectacles in order to wipe them. He could not grope about for his beloved piece of wash-leather, so he removed his hand from Lightning's shoulders in order to take his handkerchief from his trousers pocket. This action, unfortunately, caused Lightning to turn round sharply to see what John was doing. The small boy always moved and thought in that way, with a bird-like rather than a human habit of mind and body. His abrupt movement caused John to jerk the arm and drop the spectacles. As they left his hand, one of the ear-pieces caught in his finger and caused the spectacles to be thrown out, away from the rock, into the centre of the waterfall. The sudden clearing of his sight caused John to see distinctly and thus to overcome his disability. Both he and Lightning, in dismay, watched the spectacles alight on the cauldron, to be flung up on the other side of the pool without encountering anything hard. Then they gradually settled down to the bed of the stream and could be seen, trembling and wavering, on the bottom.

Before John could realize what had happened, Lightning had set his torch down on his haversack, slipped off his clothes and plunged into the centre of the pool.

John was terrified. The seething mass of water at the bottom of the fall took hold of the small white body of his companion, quarrelling over it like a nest of snakes over a captured bird. John picked up the second torch and directed both beams on to the water. He saw Lightning sucked under and thrown up again, and he tried to shout to him but was unable to make a sound from his paralysed throat. The force of the water, however, pushed Lightning out of the deep pool, and at the same moment, the boy struck out and swirled down stream for several yards, after which he regained his depth and touched the right bank. Here, he was able to stand up and turn to face John, but he had to crouch forward to withstand the rush of the stream. John could see him shivering. Above the turmoil of the fall, his voice rose, trembling like a reed:

'It's mighty cold, John, but I can make my way back.'

He proceeded to do so, battling against the river by the help of the rocky bosses and ledges along the bank, which he gripped, hand over hand, thus being able to pull himself along against the current.

John, meanwhile, focused the beams of both torches on to the pair of spectacles lying safely on the river bed.

'There they are,' he cried, no longer alarmed for Lightning's safety.

By this time, the little fellow had recaptured the distance between himself and the spectacles, and he at once saw them lying there. With a yell of triumph, he plunged in his arm and took them. In order to free his hands, he put the spectacles on his own face, a procedure which appeared to amuse him, for he burst into laughter, ignoring the fact that he had now to get back to John without being dragged by the eddy and pulled once more into the cauldron. It was not a question of distance but of height. He was not more than four or five yards away, but the water level where he had rescued the spectacles was about six feet below the ledge from which he had plunged. He had to make his way to the right-hand side of that projecting ledge, without being carried past it into the deep basin of the waterfall.

It was now that John saw the quality of the boy. He was no longer reckless: carefully judging distances, the pull of the current and the backwash of the eddy, he began to pick his way, foot by foot, with each step controlling his position by firm handhold upon the rocky bank. John followed every movement, watching with anxious eye the battle of muscle and brain against the blind force of the water. It was a beautiful scene; the toss and tumble of the fall, clothed in its own spray, the sombre indifference of the rocks, the fish-like fragility of Lightning's body, more water-sprite than human.

But John was in no mood to enjoy this purely as a picture. Indeed, he was cold with the misery of it. Could it be possible that the tiny white object, creeping along the side of the tunnel, could possibly endure for more than a few minutes? John could already foresee that as soon as Lightning relaxed his hold in order to reach up towards the ledge, the current would seize him from the waist downward, pull him back into the cauldron and drown him.

Without further reflection, he lay flat on the ledge and reached down with his stick, through the crook of which he had slipped the rope so that the noose hung out a couple of feet over the water. He had to do this with one hand while with the other he held the torch to direct Lightning to the lifeline. The boy gradually approached, and John strained himself downward, reaching as far as possible. Both made an extra effort to bridge the gap. Grunting as he did so, John gave a flick to the rope by lifting the stick a little. At the same moment, Lightning stood upright, grabbed at the noose and missed it. The movement put him at the mercy of the water, and he was thrown off his balance. Down he went, and began to swirl round towards the head of the ledge. Beyond it lay the great pool and the tumult of waters under the fall.

Then a miracle happened; or what might well be called a miracle. It was really an effort of will, but probably that is the same thing, for it means a triumph over circumstances. With instant speed, John changed over the stick and the torch, thus having the stick in his left hand. At the same time, he propelled his body leftward to the extreme edge of the rocky pier, while he shook the stick freely and was thus able to pay out a couple of extra feet of rope. The noose hit the water and was instantly worried by it, shaking and tugging at the stick in John's hand. But he kept control, and the rope lay on the water directly in the path where Lightning was being dragged back. John felt him seize it and the stick was almost dragged out of his hand. Instinctively, he put down the torch on the rock beside him and the beam of light was thus thrown, ineffectively, across the wall of the tunnel, leaving the waterfall in darkness. It

'It's mighty cold, John, but I can make my way back'

also left the struggling boy in darkness, but John could feel him securely on the end of the rope.

'Hold on!' he shouted, and with that he drew in the stick and seized the rope with both hands. The stick was now lying under him and was in his way. He wriggled back a little, and extricated it, pushing it to one side of his body. He was now firmly set on the ledge, with one foot anchored in a cleft of rock. He had the rope under him and could play it with both hands. The trouble was that he could not see because the pool beneath was in darkness, and, also, he was without his spectacles. Happily he was able to leave go with the right hand for a moment, grab the torch, and so fix it that once more its beam lit the scene of action. He saw the misty form of Lightning hanging on the end of the rope, his head above water; the situation seemed to last for hours, but, in fact, only a few moments passed before Lightning was able by the help of the rope to pull himself back to the wall and to regain his footing.

He was now safely anchored with the rope in one hand and a firm ledge of rock under the other. John flashed a torch to try to find a foothold for Lightning to lift himself out of the water and climb to the ledge. The light fell on an upturned face lit by a mischievous grin and the flashing lenses of the spectacles.

'They're quite safe,' cried the shrill voice.

'You're an imbecile,' retorted John, trying to be more savage than he felt. 'I've now got to get you up here and probably bring flowers to the funeral when you've died of pneumonia.'

'Rot,' cried Lightning. 'If you'd been fighting against the stream, you'd be as hot as I am.'

'All the more reason to get you out of it,' said John, and with that, he let down the other end of the rope and instructed Lightning to tie it loosely round his waist. Thus secured, the boy was now able to reach the ledge, and within a few minutes his skin was glowing with warmth after he had rubbed himself down with his own shirt.

John, once more in possession of his spectacles, felt it his duty still to be severe and to disguise his gratitude and admiration.

'You know,' he said, 'it's all very well, but you must realize that you are responsible to other people for your own safety.'

This solemn remark caused Lightning to lift up his voice

and crow like a cock, a reply that destroyed all possibilities of seriousness. Suddenly, in that strange scene above the waterfall, with the appalling flood slipping away into the darkness of the tunnel beyond, a peal of laughter rose from the two urchins who had yet to find a way to save themselves from destruction.

CHAPTER 12

A CROWN IN THE DUST

ALAN HOBBS insisted on leading the way when the three boys emerged from the ten-foot passage to the great cave. George made no objection, for after all, it was Alan who carried the big lamp with its beam like a searchlight. More light was what they would need as their authority, if they were to succeed in getting down to river level and rescuing John and Lightning. *If* they were to rescue them? There must be no 'if' about it; those fellows just had to be rescued. Any other conclusion was unthinkable. This meant that the boy with the best means for effecting a rescue should continue to be leader. George was content with that; indeed it never entered his head to question the matter. He fell into his place as third man, carrying his dark-lantern gingerly in the unburned hand. The other hand was clenched to ease the strain of the skin, and held up round his haversack, so that the weight of it might slow down the flow of blood in his arm, and thus ease the pain. He growled his directions, which Alan received without comment, but, nevertheless, obeyed, though in such a way that he appeared to be following his own wishes.

So the explorers tramped on, none of them in a good temper. Even Meaty was morose and had nothing to say. He was still smarting because of the snub he had received from Alan back at the shaft-head. They tramped on in silence except for the occasional husky word from the rear, giving directions. In this way, they came to the buttress where the path broke before turning left into the great transept.

Alan stopped short:

'What's this?' he said. He flashed the great beam of his lamp on it, and to George it loomed twice as big as before.

'We're beaten; the path comes to an end.'

'No, it doesn't,' growled George. 'It turns the corner on the other side of that buttress and goes into the back of the cave and then into a split in the rock face.'

'You didn't tell us of this,' said Alan, suspiciously. 'You ought to have reported it to me. I've got to think this thing out and decide what we do next.'

'You can't think that thing out,' said George, quietly. 'You've got to climb over it.'

Meaty's large body began to shake with laughter, which, out of loyalty, he tried to suppress.

'I say,' he said, 'that's a tall order. You might slip off the back of it and end up down below.'

'Up down?' snapped Alan. 'What are you talking about?'

This argument might have developed into another of his tirades against the mild Meaty, had not George cut it short.

'We must get on,' he said. 'Those chaps down below are expecting us to follow along, and I bet John will find a way through if it's humanly possible. We must be there when they do it.'

He set the example by bestriding the buttress as he had done before, and reaching up and over to the recess where he had formerly set his lantern. He was about to follow it when Alan shouted at him in tones that seemed to be convulsed with rage:

'Come back, you fool, you can't take risks like that without thinking things out.'

He was so emphatic that George, with a sigh of prolonged patience, climbed down again, only to receive a further outburst of angry remarks from the leader. When these ceased, he replied quietly: 'You see, Alan, I *have* thought things out. But it's for you to lead the way if you insist. So you go first.'

This remark, instead of soothing Alan, drove him to still further rage, which completely puzzled both the other boys.

Meaty stood in confusion and embarrassment, and might have burst into tears again had not something else happened to surprise him. And that something came from George, who became transformed from the dim follower with the dark-lantern. For a few moments, he had been watching Alan from under frowning brows, as puzzled as Meaty was. Then his eyes flashed and colour rose to his face. He, too, was angry now, but his anger released him into a fuller command, not only of himself, but of the people with him.

'Do you know what I think, Alan Hobbs?' he said, slowly and deliberately, as though each word were a blow from a clenched fist. 'Do you know what I think? I think you're bluffing. You're in a funk, and you're not fit to decide what we shall do and what we shan't do. John and Lightning have got to be rescued. We know there's a way back from here and if you want to save your skin, you can take it.'

Alan's jaw dropped. By the light of the dark-lantern which George was flashing mercilessly upon him, his tongue glistened as it flickered nervously out of his mouth and over his trembling lower lip. His eyes were clouded with confusion and fear, the fear of the coward who knows he has been caught out. But it was not in his character to admit defeat, and he quickly whipped himself up into another bout of rage.

'You're a fool,' he cried, 'how can I go back alone, past that sloping ledge? Besides, who suggested it? I didn't. I'm leading this expedition, and because I forbid what's impossible, you break out like this and start insulting me. I tell you, we've got to find another way through.'

'It's not impossible,' said George, 'and there is no other way.'

His voice was quiet again, but it had not lost its new tone of authority.

This subtle change in relationship began to affect Meaty.

He was usually upset when people quarrelled, but now he was smarting under the tongue-lashing from Alan, and he was inclined almost to take sides against him.

But his easy-going nature prevented this. Instead, he began to act on his own, leaving the others to settle their own troubles. Hitching up his belongings more securely round his mountainous person, he began to reach up with the intention of climbing over the obstacle, and thus putting it between him and the contending parties. This action, however, caught Alan's attention and gave him an opportunity, as he hoped, of slipping out of the argument and thus leaving the issue undetermined. Moreover, he saw in Meaty's action another blow to his dignity, as well as a challenge to his waning courage. This provoked another display of temper. Dodging round George, he rushed to the base of the buttress and seized Meaty by the leg, thus preventing him from mounting more than half-way up the rock.

'Come down,' he cried, his voice shrill with rage. 'You heard what I told you. You're doing it in defiance of – '

Then a dreadful thing happened. Meaty Sanders at last rebelled, and, as always happens when docile people break out, the explosion was dangerous.

'Leave go,' he growled, and there was a nasty note in his voice. That might not have mattered, had he not at the same time kicked out with his foot in an effort to shake off the grasp of Alan's hand.

The thrust was so vigorous, that his foot bounced off Alan's chest, caught the electric lamp and sent it flying out to the great cave. The beam of light threw one flashing gesture over the roof and down, for an instant singling out the hanging of rock and flesh-coloured stalactite away back in the farther reaches of the cave where the boys had entered.

There was a crash below, and instant darkness in the depths Silence followed; silence and darkness, and now the only light came from George's dark-lantern, lodged above the buttress and the edge of the platform.

Nobody moved. Meaty was still half-way up the rock, clinging there in the semi-darkness, faintly outlined by the light coming from the lantern in its niche. He knew what had happened, and he was paralysed at what he had done. Alan, too, was rigid, standing there like a king robbed of his crown. George waited. He said nothing because he still was possessed by his slowly awakened distrust of Alan. Unlike Meaty, he was obstinate once he was roused. Further, his sombre and single-track mind was still intent on his main purpose, which was to rescue his friend John and Lightning Soames.

Meaty's moment of rebellion, however, was followed by remorse. Clambering down from his perch on the buttress, he approached Alan and put an arm round his shoulders.

'Oh, Lord,' he said, 'I couldn't help it, Alan. I'm awfully sorry, Alan. Look here, you have my torch.'

And with a gesture of reconciliation, he switched on his own torch and handed it to Alan who had not moved since the catastrophe happened.

This repentance by Meaty, however, stirred him to life again, and it was not a pleasant exhibition of life. Taking the torch from Meaty, he deliberately flung it over his shoulder into the depths of the cave. He flung it so hard, that it carried backward and fell with a splash into the pool at the other end.

What he might have done next was dangerous to contemplate. The boys were now in almost total darkness, for the gleam of light peering over the top of the buttress was a feeble thing. It was enough, however, to show Alan standing with his elbows into his sides and his fists clenched together under his chin. He seemed to be struggling with some powerful opponent inside himself, some invisible demon. His eyes were staring and he appeared to be looking through the poor, repentant Meaty Sanders. The latter, and George, too, expected him to spring. But he did not; something held back that demon inside him behind the clenched fists, the staring eyes, and the hunched shoulders.

The tension was broken by George, who spoke with a merciless edge to his voice.

'That was a fool's trick,' he said, advancing slowly upon Alan. 'You've left us only my old lantern. We've got a tough job in front of us. You've forgotten that, Alan, in spite of your talk about responsibility and thinking things out. Somebody else had better do the thinking now, even though he's only got an old lantern to do it with, and to lead us down to find the other two.'

This determined speech, quite untouched by sympathy, finally broke Alan's spirit. He turned away from George, but found himself facing Meaty, and had to turn back to confront George again. He put his still clenched fists with the knuckles inward over his eyes, as though seeking to shut out humiliation. His shoulders began to shake:

'It's my father's lamp,' he said. His voice had lost its old ring. Indeed, it was little more than a whisper, for he appeared to be talking as though in a trance of fear. 'It's my father's lamp,' he repeated, 'but I didn't tell him I was borrowing it.'

With this confession, he gave up the struggle, and his two companions were shocked to see him kneel down, bury his head in his arms and sob.

This spectacle melted Meaty's heart, who now ignored the fact that Alan in a fit of temper had thrown his torch after the lamp, and thus probably endangered the lives of the whole party. For the prospect of finding a way down to the rescue of the others by the light of the old dark-lantern, was not an encouraging one. Meaty, however, for the moment forgot all this, so overcome was he by the sight of Alan kneeling in front of the buttress in misery. Meaty approached, and again put his arm round the bowed shoulders of the fallen leader.

'Look here,' he said, 'look here – '

But he could say no more; he just stood there overcome by compassion and his own good nature.

George was more practical. He was thinking of the other two fellows and their increasing danger.

'Let's get going,' he said, and once again Meaty was startled by some new quality in his voice. Perhaps Alan also noticed it for he got up meekly and stood waiting to be told what to do. George didn't tell him, however, but set an example by leading the way to the rock and mounting it. He was over the other side and standing beneath the dark-lantern before Alan's head appeared. The delay had been due to the fact that Alan had failed to get a footing up the buttress because his mind was still concerned with the problem of what his father would say when he returned home without the electric lamp. Brains as well as feet need to be on the spot when there is difficult climbing to be done.

It was not until Meaty had come up behind Alan and hoisted him up with a pair of muscular arms that the boy pulled himself together. When he got to the top and saw that the ledge both narrowed and turned into a great bay, he hesitated again. There he sat like a small child on a big rocking-horse, terrified by the fear of losing his balance.

'Come on,' said George, impatiently. But Alan did not come on. His face was on a level with the sombre gleam from the lantern, and George could see his mouth opening and shutting, though no sound issued from his throat.

George was wasting no pity on him, but suddenly he realized that the proud leader was afraid, and that fear had temporarily paralysed him. He knew, too, that this was a dangerous place in which to lose control of one's muscles. One nervous jerk might send Alan flying into the darkness, to be smashed to pulp many feet below.

George hesitated for a second; his first dark impulse was to plant a blow with his fist into that grimacing face to show how bitterly he was disillusioned. Instantly he was ashamed of this impulse. Stepping between Alan and the end of the buttress, he put himself between the boy and the fatal attraction of the abyss. Pressing two hands firmly round Alan's waist, he spoke and exerted pressure at the same time.

'Gently now,' he said, and he might have been addressing a sick child. 'You've got one leg over; lift your left leg over carefully in front of you, and you'll feel a ridge about six inches down.' Hobbs obeyed as though he were hypnotized. 'Have you got it? That's right, now turn and lean over the top and grasp that ledge below the lamp. You can let yourself down; steady now; that's right. Down a bit farther. Have you got the second ledge? Now you're on the path, step forward and let me get back for I'm too near the edge to be comfortable.'

As George moved forward, Meaty looked over the top solemnly, and his eye gleamed like that of a Negro in the light of the lamp. 'All right?' he asked. 'Then take the clobber as I pass it over.'

There followed a passage of their various properties; rucksacks and the rope ladder, sticks, tools and last and perhaps most important, Meaty's enormous nose-bag.

The rescue party gathered up this stuff and began the second stage of the journey down to floor level. George now led the way, heavily loaded. He still carried his burden in such a way that he was able to tuck his burned hand into the support of a strap across his shoulder. From the other hand hung the dark-lantern whose beam shone before them bravely enough without a rival. Meaty walked last, even more loaded than George; but he was not likely to notice that, for weights meant little to him. Besides, he was his happy self once more because his confidence in a leader had been restored, although the leader was a different one. Alan walked between them. All that he carried was the rope ladder neatly rolled and slung on his back like a rucksack. Even so, he walked as though he were heavily laden.

They trudged on in silence, directed from time to time by

a word from George who was eager to increase the pace, but was also aware that he had to conserve the strength of his party for probable difficulties in the farther cave down the slope which he had not yet explored. It was at this stage that Meaty began to hum a tune, and finally to break into song. George made no comment, but Alan walked with his shoulders even more bowed, as though Meaty were lashing him from behind with a whip.

'Dry up,' he said, at last. But Meaty went on singing, and as the three boys reached the farther bend and turned into the cleft, to disappear there, the echo of Meaty's voice floated for a moment or two in the great cave and its annexe, then fell into the prevailing silence. Only the tick-tock of the water drop from the monstrous growth in the roof broke that silence.

CHAPTER 13

HAMMER AND CHISEL

LIGHTNING appeared to be no worse for his wetting, and as soon as he had dressed, the two boys turned their attention to the problem before them. How were they to get far enough to see round that right-hand bend in the tunnel and to make sure they were not entering a trap or a blind alley? There appeared to be no answer to this question. From where they stood on the little rock jetty they could see no way ahead. The stream rushed through the tunnel lapping at both sides, and was probably both too deep and too rapid for the boys to dare an attempt at wading.

Lightning, however, had by now been able to collect his thoughts and to remember the lie of the rock down below the jetty. Suddenly, he clutched John by the coat and shook him. His voice rose to the shrill pitch that pierced the hearer's brain with its piccolo note.

'I know!' he cried, 'I know! What a fool I am not to think of it before. There's a narrow ledge just below the water level. I hung on to it when I was making my way back to you.'

'What,' said John, 'you mean that? Do you mean it's wide enough for us to find a footing?'

'I can't tell,' said Lightning. 'I put my hands out and I'm sure I felt a kind of shelf. It may not go far, but we'll try, won't we?'

He immediately became excited again and began to dance about before the light of John's torch, his wet hair stuck down and the patch of plaster on his forehead with a ring of congealed blood freshly clotted round it.

'Steady, now, steady,' said John, dropping the coil of rope over his head like a groom harnessing a wild horse. 'We shall have to take our shoes and socks off and string them round our necks.'

He had hardly spoken before Lightning was ready, and following suit himself, he decided to lead the way.

'I think we'd better rope together again,' he said, and the rope was accordingly lifted from Lightning's shoulders and shared, with a length of about six feet between the two boys.

'I don't know if we are doing the right thing,' said John with a worried look on his face. 'I've never heard my uncle talk of roping up to get through an unknown water-course. It might be dangerous if we are both thrown in, for we should get tangled with the rope if we began to struggle.'

'Stop theorizing,' said the precocious youngster. 'Let's get on or we shall freeze. The others must be waiting on the other side by now.'

'The other side of what?' asked John, who refused to allow himself to believe in an easy way out.

Between the reckless optimism of Lightning and the cautious John a means was found to get moving, and within a few minutes the two boys, roped securely together, and with their burdens packed in the top storey to avoid the wet, were feeling their way, inch by inch, along the concealed ledge of rock. It proved to be a continuous ridge about twelve inches below the surface of the stream. Their hearts were in their mouths, for a slip or a false step might mean two bodies struggling in that fierce torrent of unknown depth and strength. They pushed on, however, though within a few minutes their feet and legs were so cold that sensation almost disappeared and they might have been walking on wooden stumps. This added to the danger, because every nerve in the soles of their feet needed to be alert to a change of formation in the rock ledge. The uncertainty slowed down their progress. John had to probe in front of him with the beam of his torch, using it as firmly as a stick to examine the ledge in front of them. This was an uncertain formation, because the light of the beam tended to break up as it struck the water, revealing the rock beneath only in broken gleams almost as deceptive as the numbed sensibility in the feet that trod so gingerly behind his guidance.

Minutes passed and they seemed like hours, for the explorers' hearts were eager to get on and were impatient of this snail's progress. 'Snails!' said Lightning, his quick wits voicing his thoughts, 'more like limpets, I think.' But he was not grumbling; indeed, there was a lilt of joyous excitement in his voice. This was the kind of adventure for which he had always craved, to justify himself as a boy and not as the milksop he believed his mother and sisters were inclined to make of him. He still wanted to press on, as John could feel by the frequent slackening of the rope when Lightning edged forward nearer to him from time to time. But at each of these slackenings the leader had to warn his impetuous companion to be careful and to be sure of his footing.

'Be sensible, Lightning,' he said at last, stopping and looking over his shoulder. He dared not turn completely round. 'If you go in it means we both go and all our stuff with us. We can't afford it. We've got to keep dry, and we've got to get through this tunnel.'

He was so serious that even Lightning was reduced to discipline.

By this time, they had reached the bend. The moment came when John could flash his torch into what had been the unknown.

It was an important moment, and both boys knew it, though neither said anything to betray his anxiety. Lightning was stooping to peer under John's arm, and they stood thus like two statues.

'Good lor'!' said Lightning blankly. 'I was hoping it would be another big cave.'

'But it isn't,' said the other, with a grim note in his voice. 'It's a job now for a couple of mice, so far as I can see.' Then he added, as he leaned forward and held his torch high above his head while groping with his left hand behind him for the second one, which Lightning passed on without comment: 'And that's not very far.'

The increased light told them more of the story of what lay before them. They saw the tunnel shrinking rapidly, speeding up the flow of the stream and adding to it a touch of even greater savagery. The river growled like a wild

The moment came when John could flash his torch into what had been the unknown

animal leaping on its victim. The surface motion was broken by a criss-cross pattern of foam as the waters compressed by the sides of the tunnel were thrown closer and closer inward.

'That looks pretty ugly,' squeaked Lightning, his wet head thrust so far forward that it stuck out beneath John's arm.

John glanced down at this brave little object who seemed to be incapable of fear. He felt a glow of warmth, for courage is infectious. At his first sight of the ominous scene confronting him, he had been appalled. It looked like the end of the world, and the warning of the final darkness. The waters roared, the foam intertwisted in anger, and the walls of the tunnel prepared to close down as an impassable barrier.

'Well,' said Lightning, 'we'd better push on, hadn't we?'

But John had not recovered.

'Push on to what?' he asked gloomily. 'This looks like the end of it.'

At that he heard the voice of Lightning break into its piccolo of excitement: 'How can it be the end,' he shrieked, 'how can it? Can't you see the water rushing *through* something? It *must* be finding a way out.'

This caused John to turn himself round with care and deliberation, first one foot and then the other, to face his companion.

'You're quite right,' he said, and he was calm again; the quiet, thoughtful, bespectacled boy who went through life with a grave enjoyment, taking things as they came, and studying them with curiosity.

'We shall have to get nearer to the end,' he said, 'for I can't see, even by the two torches, what is happening there. It depends upon this ledge. If it comes to an end then we're finished, for we can't trust ourselves in that main stream. It's strong enough to drive the dynamos of a power-house.'

'Well, let's try it,' said Lightning, and he trod on John's toe as though he were already setting off.

'Steady then,' said John. That was his usual response. He lost no more time, and motioning Lightning to move carefully behind him, he began to step forward gingerly along the submerged ledge.

They proceeded thus for some fifty yards and then had to stop as the ceiling of the tunnel closed down. Another ten yards, and the boys were halted – finally, it seemed.

A wall of rock stood across the stream, hanging from the ceiling down into the water almost to the bottom. The boys knew that it could not reach quite to the bottom because the water was still rushing through, seemingly to be swallowed up into the earth. Only John could see what was happening because there was not room enough for his companion to come alongside him. He reported what he saw, how the water was suddenly deflected downwards in front of this wall, to slide away out of sight. Its anger and petulance ceased as it disappeared. The spirit of the river itself appeared to be awe-stricken by its own fate.

John concentrated the beams of both torches on that downward curve of water and succeeded in catching what he thought to be a somewhat lighter gleam about three feet below the surface.

'That's it,' he said, 'that's the edge of it. Look, Lightning! It's what they call a siphon. Explorers dive into them and trust to luck about getting out the other side.'

'I can't look,' said Lightning, 'there isn't room for me to come up alongside. Can't we change places?'

'Promise you won't do anything mad,' said John severely. 'We've got to decide very carefully what the chances are. You promise?'

'I promise,' said Lightning, and with that assurance John allowed him to edge himself round to the front place. Lightning examined the distance of the rock face below the water.

'I should say it's four feet,' he said.

'That's because you're a foot shorter than I am,' said John, and he laughed aloud.

'You're an ass,' said Lightning, who even in this dangerous pass, was touchy about his diminutive size.

As though to restore his confidence in himself, he snatched the cold chisel from his belt and reached forward to tap the rock face. *Honk, honk,* it sounded, as hollow as the voice of a wild goose in flight. He tapped again, and once more the boxy *honk, honk* rang above the growling river.

'Good Heavens,' exclaimed John, 'do you hear that? Do you hear that?'

'Hear what?' said Lightning, for even his sharp wits hadn't tumbled to the truth.

'Why, man, it's hollow, it sounds more like a drum than a rock face! That means it's only a slab of shale, a projecting fault from the roof above!'

'Yes, and what about that?' said Lightning, obligingly tapping it again and producing the tom-tom sound. Then suddenly he realized.

'Oh, glory!' he shouted, and with that he leaned farther forward to beat a tattoo on the thin face of the rock shutter. He was so excited that he over-balanced and was about to tumble headlong into the butt end of the river, to be hurled against the rock. Fortunately John was alert and had hold of the rope. Perhaps he had anticipated this characteristic outburst from the other boy.

He lay back on his heels, soaking his legs and seat in the process, braced himself against the rock and held tight. The rope pulled Lightning back with a jerk; he staggered, flopped against the wall of the tunnel, tottered forward again and then, by a miracle, recovered his balance, and was standing safely, his feet still on the ledge.

This near catastrophe, however, proved to be a help to the explorers. While stumbling, Lightning had shot one foot forward and encountered a prolongation of the shelf. It stuck out over two feet along the right-hand face of the obstruction. John worked his way past and explored this enlarged foothold.

'That's useful,' he said. The discovery more than made up for the discomfort of his wet pants and the cold which he could feel creeping up his legs during this pause for a council of action.

He stamped about with his feet, mentally taking measurements, and ascertained that he had a little platform on which to operate.

'I can work on this,' he said. 'We shall have to take it in turns and I'll start first. Now you stand behind and hold the light. We'd better have one torch only and so economize on our batteries. Give me the chisel.'

With that, he took the hammer from his own belt and began to experiment with tapping here and there across the top of the obstruction where it met the ceiling of the tunnel. Every blow rang hollow, thickening to dullness towards the nearer end.

'That means I had better start on the farther side,' he said, 'and break through the thin part first.'

'How long will it take?' said Lightning, who was not much interested in donkey work. He, too, was growing cold and John could hear his teeth chattering.

'Here,' he said, 'before we start in earnest, we'd better have something to eat.' He groped in his pocket and pulled out some wrapped barley sugars which he handed to his companion. They sucked away for some moments, but did not feel much warmer for it, for they were still standing knee-deep in the icy cold stream, and were likely to be plunged farther should they take a false step.

'Come along,' said John, at last. 'We must get down to work.'

With that, he took the chisel and hammer again from his belt and began a systematic attack, chipping first a horizontal line as far as he could reach. It was rather a feeble effort because he had not much purchase as he leaned forward, and he dared not lean too far for fear of losing his balance. It was a game needing patience, and he settled down to it as methodically as he could, knowing that so much depended upon attacking the job in the right way and not exhausting his strength too soon.

The minutes passed and lengthened into a quarter of an hour; half an hour. Lightning, who had been given John's wrist-watch to wear, looked at the luminous hands.

'It's twenty to three,' he said. 'We've been down below ground for over five hours. No wonder we're hungry!'

'Are we hungry?' said John, gasping for breath. The effort of reaching out as far as he could stretch and of chipping at the rock at the same time was already tiring him. 'Well, we'll break off for a bit and have a proper meal. I don't seem to have made much impression.'

Lightning examined the rock with both torches and re-assured him that good progress was being made. The two boys munched sandwiches contentedly, seemingly unaware of their peril.

It is astonishing how quickly a meal puts a new aspect on a difficult situation. The boys could feel themselves warming up as they devoured their cheese and tomato sandwiches and followed these up with a slab of seed cake and a swig of lemonade provided by Lightning. The consumption of this amount of food made his haversack less heavy, and, as it was impossible to remove any of their burden, this played an important part in the next stages of their struggle towards freedom.

The time was slipping away almost as rapidly as the river. Lightning looked again at the watch and found that they had spent twenty minutes on their meal. John remembered his uncle's injunction that unless the boys were home by seven o'clock he would set out with a rescue party. That sounded ignominous, and he began with renewed determination to smash his way through this first obstruction. After that, the only sounds were the music of the river, a hissing undercurrent, where the water slipped through the invisible cavity, the steady tap-tap of the hammer and chisel, and the heavy breathing of the boy labouring with them. Lightning noticed that breathing:

'Here,' he said, 'it's time I had a go. You're getting puffed, and I'm beginning to freeze up again. Let me come.'

He seized John by the shoulders as he spoke and a moment later was attacking the rock face at double the speed at which John had worked. It was useless, however, to try to slow him down. John made up his mind to let him work at his own pace and to grow quickly tired.

'Don't try to reach too far,' he said, tactfully avoiding a reference to Lightning's lack of inches. For once the younger boy did not respond by over-exerting himself. He may not have heard, for the noise of the river and the clatter of the hammer on the chisel made speech almost inaudible. Lightning was sensible enough, however, to realize that he could make more impression by working on the near, thick side of the rock face, and to this task he addressed himself with a doggedness that would have amused his companion at any other time. The present moment was not one for amusement. It was heavy with foreboding. Fatigue weighted it with lead. It carried something even heavier and colder – fear.

Standing back there against the damp wall, forcibly crouched like a coal miner at the pit-face, John studied the back of his fellow victim and was struck cold by the spectacle. What a contrast it was. The brave but feeble effort being made by one small boy against the vast immovable power which had been lying here in the depths of the earth sleeping through the ages. It had probably taken the river a million years to cut its way through this rock face. Here were two feeble human beings trying to do it in the space of an hour or two. And Heaven knows an hour or two under such conditions was likely to be unendurable. After his over-exertion he was growing cold again. He felt the chill creeping up his legs. He recollected that that was how people died, with the warmth of life ebbing from their feet upwards until it reached the heart. He shivered, and was terrified of his own fear, and the shame of it. Then a bright thought occurred to him. The effort now being made was a combination of forces. He had to look at it that way. He had to tell himself that the river had done its million years of work in preparation for him and Lightning to come along and put the finishing touch on this particular day in

September, in this particular year of grace. That was a reasonable argument and he decided to accept it. He roused himself, touched Lightning on the shoulder and said: 'My turn now. You've done a good spell.'

Lightning sucked barley sugar while John resumed his attack with the hammer and chisel. He had not been working five minutes on the farther and thin side of the face when a heavier blow made the chisel break through, leaving a hole into which they could have passed a hen's egg. It was not much progress after an hour's work, but it was enough to give them a fresh injection of courage and resolution. John could only just reach the hole but he chipped away at it and quickly enlarged it to the size of a football. After that, however, things slowed down. The rest of the surface was obstinate and John went on chipping away with little effect. He grew hot again and he could no longer reach forward to the hole, so he turned his attention to the near side where Lightning had been working. He spent a quarter of an hour on this and then had to stop. He knew that he had come to an end. He stood with his hammer and chisel raised and stared blankly at the rock a few inches in front of his eyes. He stared at it and set his jaw, and he went on staring.

'Anything wrong?' asked Lightning.

John could not reply. Had he spoken he would have turned savage; he might even have broken down and cried like a fool or a coward. Yes, a coward! That word rang in his brain. His eyes were clouded with it and he could no longer see the rock in front of him. He stood there swaying on his feet with the hammer and chisel still held up, useless before his face. He knew that little Lightning understood what was happening, or rather what was not happening, and he both blessed and cursed the knowing little character, for he was ashamed at being found out, and he was grateful for the discreet way in which Lightning took it. That is real friendship, he thought to himself, that is real friendship: to be found out, and yet still to be trusted. He was, of course, imagining all these things, and in the space of a second of time; a split second even.

'No, nothing wrong,' he said. 'I was just listening.'

It wasn't quite true, unless he meant to tell Lightning that he was listening to his own self urging him not to be defeated. But the boy took it the other way, or pretended to. John wasn't sure, but he was content to accept what might be his friend's pretence of having noticed nothing.

'Why, what can you hear?' said Lightning, his curiosity instantly aroused.

It was a curiosity which needed very little to arouse it. John continued the pretence. He even put his ear to the rock and listened solemnly. To his amazement he *did* hear something. At first he could hardly believe it and thought that Lightning was playing a trick on him. But there it was again, tap – tap!

Then – feebly – like a murmur of ghosts from the other world, there was a sound of voices through the hole which he had broken in the rock. It was so low a murmur that it sank and rose and sank again under the roar of the river. But it was voices right enough. And now it was accompanied again by a repetition of the tapping.

'What's the time, Lightning?' he shouted, his voice loud and strong and his muscles vigorous again.

'Just coming up to four o'clock,' said Lightning, 'but what can you hear?'

'I can hear voices and people tapping,' John shouted again. It was impossible to keep his voice calm. He wanted to yell and waste his strength, but he made an effort and regained control of himself. 'We've got three hours more,' he said.

With that, he beat a tattoo on the rock face with his hammer and got an immediate response from the other side. He shone the torch right through the hole and heard a muffled cheer. He and Lightning replied lustily. That was all. It was not yet time for rejoicing. John attacked with hammer and chisel and with each blow he felt the vibration of the responding blow from the other side. He realized that somebody was at work with intelligence, and he knew that it must be George. He, too, had learned something more about human nature that day.

CHAPTER 14

THE OTHER SIDE

MEATY SANDERS stopped singing half-way along the passage to the farther cavern. It was not a place to be merry in. With the tips of the fingers a man could touch each wall, and this narrow corridor reaching up to what might be infinity made a human being crawling along the base of it feel himself to be something smaller than an ant. It killed sound, too. Meaty heard his voice come back on him like the slap of wet flannel; a most discouraging experience.

'I say!' he said, and after this lugubrious remark he relapsed into silence.

Thud, thud of boots on the rock and an occasional sigh when Alan Hobbs drew a deep irregular breath; these were the only sounds that rose above the gradually increasing murmur of the hidden stream.

It was uncomfortably dark, a fact which served to keep Alan's outbursts of temper constantly in the minds of his companions. What would happen now if the oil in the dark-lantern gave out? It was a question that began to haunt both George and Meaty; George especially, because he knew what a shaky affair was his contribution to the lighting scheme of the whole expedition. This, apart from other considerations, made it urgent for the boys to press on. George was not too cheerful about the prospect. His burnt hand was stinging and he was tired and hungry, for he had already done this journey once; but he was too worried about the rest of the party to permit himself to suggest stopping for a meal, though he knew that Meaty would welcome such a proposal. He compromised:

'We'd better eat something as we go along.'

'I couldn't care more!' was the response from the rear,

and the party emerged from the passage on to the narrow gallery of the farther tunnel to the sound of eager rummaging in Meaty's enormous nosebag.

'Coming up,' said a cheerful voice, and George found a sausage roll thrust into his hand, a kindness which made him wince because the undamaged hand was the one holding the lamp. Alan received his share, too, but he was still not in a condition to thank anybody.

Two of the three boys stood munching ravenously for five minutes.

'Well now,' said George, 'we daren't wait any longer. We must eat as we go.' Meaty responded by handing round cheese sandwiches, and hoisting his gear into position. George led the way again, taking the left-hand branch of the gallery and picking his way carefully down its sloping surface.

'We come to a drop in a few minutes,' he said, 'and that's as far as I reached. The last man down will have to unhitch the short rope, or we may do it by means of the rope ladder. I reckoned it was about fifteen feet, and there is a knob of rock at the top round which we can throw a double loop of rope.'

He had hardly finished speaking when they reached the spot. The drop accentuated the darkness and the little dark-lantern flickered. Two hearts jumped, but the flame recovered itself and shone a little brighter than before. Perhaps the wick was shedding a crust. George prayed that it might be so. He dared not shake the lantern to test the oil level for fear he put the flame out. The thing was to get down this drop as soon as possible.

If the worst happened after that they would at least have this grey film of daylight to lead them down to the floor of the cave. An encouraging murmur came up from the stream.

The difficulty was that George dared not tilt the lantern; therefore the illumination of the drop of fifteen feet was only a sort of penumbra on the outskirts of the feeble beam that hit the wall of the cave across the little chasm.

What made the prospect worse was the helplessness of Alan Hobbs. He appeared to be moving in a trance. He still carried half a sausage roll and an untouched sandwich in his hand and he had hardly spoken a word since the boys had set off from the great buttress.

'We'll have the rope ladder,' George said to him, expecting him to respond at once. But he stood there with the rolled ladder on his back, and the food in his helpless hand. He stared at George blankly.

'Come on, Alan,' said George, sharply. 'The rope ladder!'

But it was Meaty who answered by gently lifting the ladder over Alan's head and beginning to unfasten it while the helpless boy stood trembling.

'It's my father,' he said. 'When he gets in a temper it's frightful. I can't tell him I've lost the lamp.' His voice shook and his trembling increased.

His trouble was so apparent that not even the darkness could hide it. George and Meaty looked at each other quickly. They realized that here was another and even more serious liability. It was useless to bully the poor fellow, for his mind was sick.

'Let's think about that when we get out,' George said. He spoke quietly, while unrolling the ladder down the side to the ledge fifteen feet below.

'Here,' he added, giving the end of the short rope to Alan. He hoped it would be long enough. 'Get busy with this and help us to turn a double loop round this boss of rock so that the two ends can hang down for us to unhitch the whole thing from below.' They now had a double turn of rope round the rock on which they hung the top hooks of the ladder.

'I'll go first,' said Meaty. 'If it bears me it will bear anything.'

A moment later he was over the edge among the rungs

of the ladder. It gave a loud squeak, and Alan on one side of the boss and George on the other, held firmly to the rope attaching it to the rock.

'O.K.,' shouted Meaty, 'it bears. I'm going down now.'

The ladder protested under the weight but in a few moments Meaty was down and had found a safe footing on the ledge below.

'Throw your end of rope down to him,' said George; suiting the action to the word, but Alan was still not functioning properly, for George had to take the rope out of his hands and throw it down to Meaty, who shouted up cheerfully:

'Come on, Alan, I'm holding on tight down here to the rope.'

Alan appeared to understand neither the mechanics nor the command, and George prompted him, telling him to go next; but he did not obey. Instead, he began to tremble again, and could be heard breathing like someone snoring in sleep. George thought quickly. This was a new experience and something resolute had to be done. He had a flash of inspiration which enabled him to read the troubled page of Alan's mind.

'Come on, Alan,' he said, 'forget all that. We'll get John's doctor uncle to tell your father about the lamp. It was an accident after all.'

'Yes, but I didn't ask him for it! I took it without asking,' whispered Alan, still in a state of semi-trance. 'You don't know what he's like when he's angry.'

'We've got other things to face first,' said George, a little more firmly. 'You must forget your troubles for a bit and think about John and Lightning. It's our job to get them out of this. I believe we may find a way down to the bottom here, and we've got no time to lose so you must pull your weight.'

This matter-of-fact approach sobered Alan somewhat, and he made an effort to return to the situation in hand.

'All right,' he said, 'you go next.'

'No,' said George, 'I'm coming last. Look, I'll help you over the edge. Now, take it slowly.' It was an odd thing, but all his anger against Alan evaporated as he took him under the armpits and felt his body still trembling.

Alan permitted himself to be guided to the edge, where he groped with his feet until he had found the rungs of the ladder. He was still in such a shaken condition that George was half afraid to leave go; but this was no time for sentiment. The minutes were slipping away dangerously. A few more of them passed while Alan went down, rung by rung, like an old man. The boy remaining at the top saw in the thin light that Meaty received the burden safely. He then prepared himself, taking the lantern in his damaged hand and swinging himself over the edge to grasp the ladder with the other. Holding the lantern was an agony that made George sweat, but he went down slowly and as soon as he reached the bottom he instructed Meaty to pull on the right-hand rope-end.

Both rope and ladder came tumbling down to be rolled and restored to the pack. The party then continued downwards with George still in the lead.

As they set off, he turned his head to look down across the cave to the constantly changing shape of light in the bed of the stream. From his new position, half-way down the wall of the cave the opening into what must be the outer world looked larger. He was so fascinated by it that he stopped walking and was bumped into by Alan, who drew up with a start of surprise as though he had been shaken out of a deep sleep.

'You see that?' said George, thinking this is a good way to put some courage into the unhappy boy. But Alan was not interested. He merely put out his hand and touched George in the small of the back, as though dumbly urging him on, or groping his way in a dream. George gave up the effort to console him, and proceeded with the descent.

As they neared the floor of the cave, the thin film of daylight grew slightly stronger. It revealed the lower reaches of the gigantic walls, and touched the waters of the stream with a glint like that of a mole's coat. Nature had taken advantage of this shadow land, and the boys could see around them masses of fungi like mildewy biscuits, stuck edgewise on the walls. On a boss of rock breaking the smoothness of the floor where it approached the aperture, there was even a growth of pale vegetation, creeping out of a bed of moss in long tendrils like white runlets of oil, seeking the light.

The various objects were signs of life. To creatures for ever doomed to a life in the underworld they would have been promise of something better to come, in another world, just as human beings in the moments of earth's greater glories, find promises of something beyond their understanding.

Meanwhile, this slight change of condition appeared to affect Meaty Sanders favourably, for he began to hum to himself as he brought up the rear on that steep path down the ornamented walls of the cave. And when Meaty hummed to himself, it was equivalent to any other boy singing in a choir. Rummaging could be heard in the nosebag, and soon the music was punctuated by bumping sounds, like that of a trumpet being muffled while in full blast. It was Meaty adding another course to his late luncheon.

The beam of the lantern was diluted by the twilight and suffered a chemical change. It was now of a dull orange hue, and the draught blowing immediately down the stream caused that orange flame to flicker from time to time with a suffusion of blood-red smoke. Was this a sign of expiry, or was it due merely to a change of atmosphere? George glanced anxiously at the lamp.

It had brought them safely to the very threshold of freedom, or what promised to be freedom; was it, like Moses, about to die within sight of the promised land? The flame answered the question for him by suddenly breaking into a spluttering and spitting. Then it went out. He stared at it in dismay, and watched its soul depart in a little spiral of smoke, ghostly white in the twilight.

This brought the boys to a standstill again and they stood in Indian file wondering what to do next.

'Oh, Lord,' said Meaty, and he choked on an extra large mouthful before he could add: 'Now we're for it!' Neither he nor George mentioned the torch which Alan had wilfully thrown to its destruction. The culprit said nothing, so what might have been going on in his conscience remained hidden from the others, and perhaps even from himself, for he still appeared to be incapable of thought or free action.

'We can see all right,' said George, as soon as their eyes had grown accustomed to the dimness. 'Let's push on, for we're near the bottom and ought to be able to trace where this water's flowing from. It must connect somehow or other with the bottom of the pot-hole where we left John and Lightning. Come along, Alan.' He spoke almost kindly; and, indeed, that was the attitude of both boys to the former leader of the expedition. He seemed to have got so far beyond the stage of being sorry for himself, that other people had to be sorry for him.

The slope increased its angle and the last few yards were covered by three figures half sliding and half stooping to keep their balance. The floor of the cave proved to be loose of surface, a mess of broken shale and gravel spotted with fungi and fragments of moss, some of them oozing moisture which they had captured, perhaps, from the occasional outbreaks of spray from the flowing water of the river. George trod on one of these patches and it squelched under his foot and appeared to turn black in the half light.

These details, however, attracted only small attention from the adventurers, because they were eager to explore the back of the cave. They had not far to seek, for the curve of the wall was not deep, and the boys found that they had reached the floor almost at the water's edge, within ten feet of what appeared to be a huge slit in the rock, about six feet wide and a foot deep, out of which the water poured as from the mouth of one of the gigantic figures in a Roman fountain. At first sight, this seemed final and George stared gloomily at it. Nobody could possibly get through that aperture. It was dead and black, suggesting that the conduit had been bored through impassable masses of rock which lay, tomb-like, between the rescue party and their imprisoned friends.

George did not despair, however. The other boys saw him frown, and the frown grow into a savage scowl that made him quite frightening. He clenched his fists and impatiently prodded his hips with them as though urging himself to spring bodily through the solid rock.

'What do we do now?' said Meaty.

'Eh?' George growled like an angry dog. Before he could reply, Meaty interrupted again with a howl of delight.

'The candles,' he shouted, 'we've forgotten the candles!' And he plunged his arm into the rucksack of which he had relieved himself while they were standing still. He produced a bundle of half a dozen and handed one to each of the other boys. By this light, they proceeded to examine what appeared to be a hopeless situation. There shone the implacable wall of rock with its little knots of moss and fungi, almost mockingly pretty. George's frown suddenly cleared. He held his candle above his head and looked intently at a spot about four feet above the water. Then he approached, and snatching the hammer from his belt, began to tap the spot: 'We've got something here,' he said. His voice was quiet and thoughtful; 'This looks to me like a flaw and we may be able to cut it away.'

With this he divested himself of his burdens, first fondly putting his dark-lantern down in a spot where it would not be forgotten, which was possible as it no longer played a part in the scheme of things. Then he took off his coat, folded it up and laid it on the rest of the clobber. Meaty watched him thoughtfully and stared at the tattered lining of the coat. He glanced up from this to the rock face above the open mouth through which the river poured.

'It seems to me,' he said, 'that I'd better get across to the other side of the water and make a start there. We've got two hammers and two chisels.'

With this, he drew the tools from his own belt and tossed them across the stream. They fell damply and something scuttled away on clockwork wheels. It was a rat.

'Look! Signs of life,' shouted Meaty. He was so excited that he seized Alan round the waist and lifted him bodily from the ground. Then abashed at what he had done, he put his late leader down almost gently, but even so he could not refrain from jubilation. Singing aloud, he took a flying leap at the narrowest part of the stream and landed safely on the other side, wetting only one leg which slipped from the bank and touched the water. Within an instant, he had picked up hammer and chisel and was tapping away like a woodpecker.

Meanwhile, George went more methodically to work, bringing a candle-flame to examine the curious shutter of rock that might have been let down to within a foot of the bed of the stream, like the safety curtain in a theatre. A rusty stain of iron zigzagged across, and it occurred to him that this might be due to thinness by decomposition, and that the right place to attack was at the top of this flaw.

He looked round and found Alan still standing idle. It was better to give the poor fellow something to do.

'Here,' he said, 'lend a hand. Hold the candle with the light over my left shoulder, while I get to work.'

Meaty, who had stopped prospecting in order to light another candle and set it up in a little recess, was now hard at work again and for the next quarter of an hour the rhythmic tapping of two hammers on two cold chisels was unbroken. Alan held the candle aloft, changing hands from time to time as one arm grew numbed. At the end of the first spell, he was shivering with cold, so George turned to him, gave him the tools and showed him precisely where to continue work. The resultant rhythm was different, lop-sided, for while Meaty continued untiringly hammering at

Then he began to tap the spot

the place where he had started, Alan worked more uncertainly, slowing up from time to time, his attention wandering. Finally he stopped and George said with some show of impatience:

'Come on, Alan, we've got to break through. Are you getting tired?'

'No,' Alan replied, his voice still monotonous and remote,

as though he were half a mile away. 'No,' he repeated, 'I only forgot. You see, it's something more than temper. It's as though he goes really mad when anything goes wrong. My mother says – '

'Look here,' said George, 'you're letting this get on your mind. Everybody has to face the music at some time or other. I don't always find life easy myself.'

He smiled grimly, and the candlelight showed lines in his face that made him appear to be wearing the mask of old age. 'We've got to think now how John and Lightning are feeling. It must be hell behind that rock. Don't you realize that they are trapped?'

His own question roused him to a fresh display of obstinate determination. Snatching the tools from Alan's nerveless hands, he renewed his attack on the rock face, while Alan resumed command of the candle, the sweat running down his face.

So the work went on, and time passed without bringing much encouragement to the rescue party. The three candles burned lower and, at last, the one which Meaty had set in the niche subsided and went out. He stopped work, to strike a match in order to find it. George stopped too, turning to look across the water inquiringly. The resultant silence was uncanny. The river began to murmur again as it rushed from the dark mouth to the light one across the floor of the cave. Another rat scuttled about, unseen. There was a splash as it took to the water.

'What's that?' said Alan, quickly, and he switched round to face the rock where the work was in progress.

'Another rat,' said Meaty, laconically, while he set up the candle in the niche and relit it.

'Not that,' said Alan. He seemed suddenly to have wakened up. 'It's not the rat I mean. Can't you hear it?'

'Hear what, man?' said George irritably. He thought Alan was showing off again after regaining confidence, and he was suspicious of him.

'It's on the other side,' cried Alan, and he was so excited that his voice cracked and rose to a thin scream.

'Steady now,' said George. 'Keep hold of yourself.'

'But I tell you – '

Then Alan stopped, and stooping, put his ear to the damp rock face. Reaching out a hand and beckoning, he drew George to him, who likewise put an ear to the rock. They both crouched there for several moments. Then George rose, stretched his back and stared thoughtfully at the incisions which he and Meaty had made.

'Yes,' he said quietly, 'I can hear it. It's John at work on the other side. We must go steady now. We know they're there, and we've got to work on till we get them out.' He looked keenly at Alan and gave his orders. 'Meaty and I are breaking off for some food. You carry on, meanwhile, partly to help with the work and partly to let them hear that we're behind the rock face.'

Nobody questioned his command, nor the way in which he had reacted to the good news. Meaty threw a packet of sandwiches across the stream and both boys refreshed themselves. Ten minutes later, Alan paused for breath, but the sounds did not cease, for the tapping from the other side could now be heard distinctly. Where before it had been on the hither side of the water, it now came from the spot where Meaty was working, and the sound was more of a scrape than a tap, as though made with a chisel at an acute angle which caused the tool to slip slightly at each blow, like a skid which the tip of a billiard cue makes on the ball under a false stroke.

All three boys stared at the spot where the sound appeared concentrated. Meaty was about to pop the last of the sandwich into his open mouth, when his hand was arrested and his great loose lips hung apart while his eyes goggled. For there, within a few inches of the marks he had made in the rock, a lump of shale suddenly fell, then another; then a pad of moss broke away and hung down like a turned cuff. The exposed surface flaked still farther, then broke and a hole appeared. With a mighty roar, Meaty lifted up his voice and shouted. The result was that the hole in the rock appeared to blink like an eye. Yes! it really shone, throwing a ray of light that made a little pattern across the angle of the cave in the same shape as the recently made hole. Somebody was directing the beam of a torch through that hole.

All three boys raised a cheer and a moment later they heard a little trickle of sound which they recognized as a responding cry from John and Lightning.

CHAPTER 15

REUNITED

AFTER that it was work, and still more work, the party on one side of the barrier competing with the other in eagerness to be the first to crash through. The minutes passed swiftly, but not swiftly enough for Lightning, who could be heard through the hole in the wall as he urged John to still greater effort, or took a turn himself with such frantic speed that he was quickly exhausted and had to relinquish the tools to his steady companion. After a while, the work was more carefully co-ordinated. John had an idea that brought good results. He shouted through to George, directing that the attack with hammer and chisel should be synchronized, the chisel on one side working within a few inches of that on the other. This had a scissor effect and doubled the rate of progress. At half-past four, the screen of rock began to tremble violently under the blows.

'Stop!' shouted George, and the hammering ceased. He studied the obstacle with a critical eye, observing how the chisels had eaten their way in the shape of an arch. He made up his mind.

'Have you room to stand back there?' he shouted. 'We're going to try to push it down.'

John's voice answered him. It sounded weak, as though the poor fellow, who had done most of the work on his side, were near the end of his strength.

'Plenty of room,' he said, 'we've only to stand aside on the ledge. But mind you don't tumble through or you'll land in deep water immediately under the rock where the river has burrowed.'

'Right then,' shouted George. His voice had lost its

huskiness and had taken on a cheerful ring. 'I shall count one . . . two . . . three!' Then he turned to Meaty:

'Now, Meaty, you from your side and I from mine with the soles of our boots! We'll give a hearty push together when I say "three"!'

Alan butted in. He had picked up a lump of rock, half the size of a small paving stone:

'I'll hurl this into the middle of it as you kick,' he said.

George looked at him with surprise; it was the first sign of initiative he had shown since the loss of his lamp.

'All right,' he said, and oddly enough his voice was husky again. It was as though he were returning to his old self.

Now came the critical moment.

'One . . . two . . . three . . . *at it*!'

The blows of two stout legs and a heavy lump of rock were beautifully timed. They came with one solid thud.

The screen cracked along the top, then split down the middle and collapsed like two wings being furled. There was a splutter of fragments of wet moss, a roar as the waters received the debris, and then the river flowed on through an open gateway, while the rescue party looked into the darkness and saw the faint outline of two figures seemingly clinging to the wall of a tunnel with their feet just below the surface of the water.

Nobody moved. The excitement had been so great, and the last half-hour of labour so intense, that the relief embarrassed everybody. There was a gap of nearly three feet between the submerged pier on which John and Lightning were standing and the broad bank from which the rescue party had worked. George was the first to recover from the inaction. Stepping forward, he reached out his right arm through the opening, saying as he did so:

'Dr Livingstone, I presume.'

This remark caused John and Meaty to break into laughter; an event which puzzled Alan and Lightning, who apparently were not so strong on history. The laughter, however, was followed by a howl of pain from George, for John had grasped his hand firmly, expecting to leap the gap.

'What on earth's the matter?' asked John.

'Oh! I burnt my hand on my old lantern.'

'Where is it now?'

'It's gone out; run out of oil.'

'What about the rest of your lights?' asked John, leaning forward and peering into the outer cave, expecting to see the beam of the big electric lamp.

Before George could explain further, he was interrupted by Alan who spoke up sharply and with almost a complete return of the old authority in his voice.

'Look here,' he said, 'let's get on with it. It's turned half-past four and we could all do with something to eat.'

He took the position from which George had stepped back and proffered his hand, gave a firm pull and brought Lightning across the gap. John followed and the rescue party could now see that both boys were nearly exhausted. They were shivering after being almost knee-deep in the icy stream for so long under conditions of heavy anxiety and labour.

'Now then,' said Alan, determined once more to be commander of the enterprise. 'These fellows need a hot drink.'

It was a good move on his part, because a hot drink was precisely what their rescued companions wanted, and to suggest it served to restore Alan, at least in his own eyes, to his former position as president of the Tomahawk Club.

The picnic basket, which so far had remained intact, and had been carried about by George, was now put into service. Meaty lit the spirit lamp, filled the saucepan with water from the river, added milk and cocoa, and soon a fragrant smell arose and a cup of boiling drink was handed to each member of the party.

Meanwhile, John and Lightning had rubbed their feet

back to life. The next job was to get shoes and socks on to their swollen feet again, for the boys could not walk bare-footed. It was done at last, however, and after everybody had eaten and finished off the cocoa, the adventurers were ready for the last stage of their journey in the underworld.

While Meaty was packing up, he spoke to himself, but loud enough to be heard by the others.

'Hm!' he muttered, 'that veal pie went down all right; and the sausage and tomatoes, too. Pity we could not tackle the salmon; means I've got to take it home again.'

He shook his head thoughtfully as he put the unused tin back into his rucksack. 'Those peaches were pretty good, though!'

His soliloquy was interrupted by Alan, who spoke up boldly again:

'Well, now, it's ten past five, we ought to be getting on. Shall I lead the way?'

It was George who replied. He was studying Alan's face intently. He was puzzled. 'Lead the way?' he queried. 'It's only as far as that outlet.' And he pointed with his stick to the flickering oval shape at the other end of the cave where the light from the outside world shone like the wall of an aquarium.

'What do you mean?' said Alan, turning on him suspiciously.

'We'd better go and see, we don't know what the position is yet.'

They crossed the floor of the cave along the right-hand bank of the stream and peered down into the luminous hole. The edges of it were softened here and there with clumps of water-weed which fluttered in the current like flags in a high wind. Bottle-green and mole-coloured, these masses of weed were truly flowers of the underworld. From time to time, a single fish flickered out of the darkness into the circle of light and disappeared, its body being caught into transparency. Suddenly, a dozen, then a hundred fish, rust-spotted trout, rushed through, their skeletons showing like shadows within the flesh, and the flesh no more than a gleam of cold fire.

John looked at George, and saw him gazing entranced at the marvellous picture. The light was glinting up from the hole into his face, throwing over it a constantly flickering glow. For a moment George, too, might have belonged to the people from another world. It was he who broke the spell:

'What do you think of that, John?' he said, dipping his stick into the water to test the depth.

'It's what they call a siphon,' John explained once again. 'It means that the roof dips down below the surface of the water. It was the same with the gap we've just come through, only there it is thin and deep, while this one is long and shallow.' He paused, looked from George to Alan shrewdly, then added: 'It means that this is a safe way out, but we've got to dive through it, a matter of about four or five feet, I should say, judging by the light coming through.'

'What about our things?' demanded Meaty looking ruefully at his luggage.

'We shall have to tie everything up in our mackintoshes and trundle the bundles through as though we were playing water polo. We can use the long rope and have all the bundles in a line like the tail of a kite. The first man can take the end of the rope and once he's through he can pull the bundles as we manoeuvre them from this side. Is that agreed?'

'Rather,' cried Lightning, who was freshly galvanized by his good meal, and was ready to throw sparks in all directions once his excitable imagination was touched. 'I'll go first with the rope end.' For a second time that day he began to strip off his garments.

Meanwhile, George had satisfied himself that the water was about four feet deep between the top of the opening and the bed of the stream, and that the top was about a foot below the surface, thus making the river about five feet deep in all.

'That seems simple enough,' he said. 'We ought all to be through in a quarter of an hour, with everything high and dry.'

Perhaps he and John had been making these deliberations while secretly watching Alan, for they showed no surprise when he began to betray signs of uneasiness that rapidly developed into another of those tell-tale fits of temper. As usual, he vented it on the innocent Meaty, who was quietly preparing himself for the plunge through to daylight.

'What are you doing?' Alan shouted, his voice harsh and broken. 'It's impossible! We're risking our lives, as well as spoiling everything we've got.'

'What do you suggest, then?' said George, quietly. He looked at John as though appealing to him for support.

'What do I suggest?' said Alan, but now his voice was trembling. 'There is no suggestion about it, we've got to go back the way we came.'

'You mean we must negotiate those two difficult bits, the fifteen-foot drop up there,' he pointed to the flaw in the ledge near the top of the cavern, 'and the place in the first cave where we had to rope together?'

This reminder drew Alan to a further display of anger. He stamped his foot and almost screamed in his effort to intimidate the rest of the party.

'I don't care what we've got to do, I won't allow us to take this risk, even though you don't want to face the journey back. I can't swim, for one.'

This confession was seized upon by the merciless little imp, Lightning Soames.

'Can't swim?' he mocked. 'How's that?' His disbelief was so sincere that it sobered Alan who began to explain.

'I went for a lesson with my father once, and he threw me in the deep end, when I wasn't looking, and my mother would not let me go again.' Then he resumed his air of command; 'But that's nothing to do with it; I say we've got to go back.'

'It's everything to do with it,' said John, who had been looking on in bewilderment at what, for him, was this first outburst of Alan's temper; 'If you can't swim, you can't; though I should have thought you might have held your breath, hung on to the bundles, and be hauled through. But perhaps that's expecting too much.' He thought for some moments, then added: 'Well, I suppose there's no help for it; it's a case of the weakest link in the chain. But where's your lamp, Alan?'

This question, again asked apparently in all innocence by the matter-of-fact John, had a strange effect. It turned everybody to stone, even including Lightning who stood like a little naked statue with his shirt in his hands. Nobody spoke; nobody looked at anybody else. George broke the spell.

'His lamp's gone.' He sounded shame-faced. 'There was an accident, and his lamp went over the edge. That's all. But we had to carry on with my old lantern, and now that's run dry.'

'But Meaty had a torch,' said John. He was a great fellow for getting the facts right.

Alan could stand this inquisition no longer.

'Go on, tell them,' he shouted, his voice cracking again, 'tell them all about it! Tell them exactly what happened!' And for the second time that day he fell on his knees and hid his face in his arms, sobbing hoarsely.

'That would be a long story,' said George, 'and if we are going back we ought to start at once. So let's get moving, Alan.' He turned to the others: 'And the rest of you: let's get moving. Come along.'

He began loading himself up and stood waiting while Lightning put his clothes on again with a demure obedience.

Nothing more was said about attempting the dive through the siphon. Indeed, nothing was said at all because of the general embarrassment at seeing Alan so humiliated. Everybody was now waiting for him, and when at last he looked up he saw all four of them standing with their packs on their backs. He followed suit but with his back turned to them, loading himself with the rope ladder and one of the axes.

'John, you lead the way,' said George. He was obeyed instantly.

Once more they moved off in Indian file towards the foot of the sloping ledge at the back of the cave where the stream emerged. Before they reached it, however, Lightning, with his bird-bright eye, spotted something which caused him to break rank and to dart diagonally across the cave to the wall almost directly under the opening at the top, where the rescue party had entered. His voice was shriller than ever with excitement:

'Look here,' he cried; 'Look! Look! Another way through.'

The rest of the party scrambled after him, all discipline forgotten. Before they could reach him he had disappeared into an opening about half his own height, and they saw a trickle of sand run out where his boots had scraped the floor within. John followed and by the light of his torch, saw that he stood in another irregular corridor sloping up towards the interior. In a moment, he had produced his own compass and taken a bearing. The corridor led northward, which meant that it must reach up either to the floor of the first cave or to one beyond it.

Time was forgotten, for this new turn of events might solve the problem of facing those three difficult obstacles in the return journey; the fifteen-foot drop, the great buttress, and the broken ledge. So George thought, as he knelt behind John and peered along his back at Lightning's disappearing form.

'Carry on, then,' he said quietly, 'don't let him get out of sight, or he may get into trouble again.' Then he called over his shoulder: 'Alan, you come next, and let Meaty bring up the rear.'

Lightning, who was really very tired and had lost his india-rubber-like quality, waited for the others to overtake him, and the party went on, united but silent. The corridor continued to be sandy, which was fortunate as they had to go forward on hands and knees and were grateful for the soft floor. John's larger torch had been handed forward to Lightning, and Meaty had lighted a candle to use as a tail-light to the procession. They made good progress, steadily rising until they came to a point where the corridor broke into two. They stopped again and both compasses were produced to take another bearing. The right-hand fork pointed north-east, and the left-hand fork, north-west.

'What do you think?' said Lightning after a quizzical glance at John's compass.

'The right-hand one should lead up to the big cave,' said John. 'Where the other one goes we don't know, but surely it must roughly follow the stream and should thus bring us out to the open air.'

'How long have we got?' cried Lightning.

'It's half past five, now.'

'Then we've time for a peep at the big cave,' cried Lightning, dancing about again with renewed energy: 'Come along, all of you, let's get cracking.'

He had begun to dance off along the right-hand passage, when George thrust out an arm and barred the way.

'No,' he said. That was all. Everybody waited again, and after frowning heavily, as though struggling to find words to express his thoughts, he added slowly: 'We've had enough for one day. We need a bit of margin of time, for we don't know where this other path leads yet. There may be trouble ahead. Besides, you two have had a good wetting and you ought to get home and change.' There was another pause and his face became almost contorted with the effort to find words. He clenched his hands and they saw him wince with pain. They also saw him look at his bandaged hand as though a bright idea had struck him, a real inspiration and way out of his difficulty.

'That's enough! We don't want any more explanations. There are other reasons why we should get out of this.' He looked shyly at Alan, who was standing hunched under the rope ladder. 'Let's say I've burnt my hand and it's infernally painful. I forgot to see to it when I got back to the first-aid box, and it's gone stiff. Just as well to get out and see what the damage is.'

John had seen that shy glance at Alan, and putting two and two together he knew that there was something behind all this, and that George had thought up a convenient excuse for putting an end to the day's work. John said nothing, however. There was a quality in George's manner which forbade argument; nor, indeed, did John want to disagree with him, for he was fagged out after his labour at the rock face while standing knee-deep in the icy stream.

'We take the left-hand path,' said George. Without further comment Lightning led the way, followed by the rest of the team. The unexplored path leading into the interior of the labyrinth of caves, remained an unanswered riddle, perhaps for future reference.

CHAPTER 16

SUNSET

THE left-hand tunnel rose fairly steeply, then dropped with an abruptness that alarmed the weary explorers, who began to fear that the way out was not so near as they had hoped. The sandy floor was replaced by bare rock, and this added to their difficulties. However, they reached the bottom of the slope only to find that the next stage was a switchback journey on rapid undulations where the tunnel made its progress over and under the great blocks of rock formation building up the interior of the hills.

It was rough going, and the explorers were neither in mood nor physical condition to take it cheerfully. The corridor now began to wind about, and this destroyed their sense of direction. Finally George called a halt while he and John consulted the compass again. They were still heading north-west.

'We'll carry on then,' said George. 'So long as we follow this direction we are bound to reach daylight.'

Once again they resumed their way, a silent band, crawling on hands and knees for another fifty yards. Then the corridor suddenly gave them head room and they were able to walk upright. This had a cheering effect and Lightning began to run forward, shouting that he would find the exit and report back. But George fiercely recalled him and with instant docility he returned to his place at the head of the column. John followed him, plodding along in silence, his face a blank behind those studious spectacles. He was nearing the point of exhaustion, but would not admit it even to himself. He could hear Alan slouching along behind him, a broken figure. Meaty was the most cheerful because he had the greatest reserve of physical strength, and a nature willing to allow others to take responsibility. Meaty was last man and therefore only he could observe George, either the way he walked or the way he was thinking.

Everybody knows what it is to reach that moment in a journey or on a job when all the spirit and fun drop out of it. The mind begins to question every detail and even the purpose of the whole enterprise. How many undertakings are given up at this stage nobody knows, because such things are usually not mentioned. One thing is certain; these dark misgivings always come before the moment of glory.

So now it was. Even Lightning was walking with bent head and a limp. From time to time, he put up his hand to the plaster on his forehead as though suspecting it to have changed into a lump of lead. The floor of the corridor was once more carpeted with sand, so that the footsteps of the five boys made a muffled sound. On they went, shuffle, shuffle, the light of the first torch mopping and mowing with a monotonous regularity.

Then something happened. At one of the downward beats of the beam of light in Lightning's hand, the illumination swept along the floor and struck a small round object. Lightning was about to kick it when John suddenly woke up, seized him by the shoulder and held him back.

'For Heaven's sake!' he cried.

The boys crowded round the little object lying in the sand at their feet. Meaty brought his candle flame and they examined the find more closely, nobody daring to touch it after the warning from John. It was a skull. It lay half buried in sand; near it, rose several ridges which might denote other bones. John knelt down reverently and scooped away the sand from around the skull. Certainly it was a human skull, though the jaws and teeth were somewhat ape-like.

'What have we found?' murmured John, to himself. He was trembling with excitement, and the other boys looked on amazed. 'Don't you see,' he said, 'it must be incredibly ancient! There's no sign of any recent disturbance here: no footprints, no shreds of clothing, nothing at all except this. It may have been here ten thousand years. You've heard of the Piltdown skull, haven't you?'

He asked this question as though quoting Holy Scripture. But none of the other boys had heard of the Piltdown skull, and John sighed because of the burden of responsibility which his knowledge put upon him. 'It's probably a relic of primitive man,' he said, 'and *we* have discovered it!'

'Well, what do we do now?' cried Lightning. 'Shall we wrap it up and take it with us?'

John shuddered at the idea of such sacrilege. He appealed to George who had been looking on in silence.

'We mustn't touch it,' he said. 'We must leave it exactly as it is for the expert archaeologists to see how it is lying and precisely where. All we can do is to make a note of its position and how to get to it. My uncle will know what to do after that.'

John's earnestness and George's air of quiet authority compelled obedience. Within a few minutes, George had drawn in his sketch-book a diagram showing the position of the skull, and he followed this by making a drawing of it, carefully measuring so that he would get all the proportions right. After that, the boys carried on along the corridor, counting their paces and noting the distance on the diagram. This preoccupation almost banished fatigue. It also made them fail to notice that from beyond a curve in the tunnel ahead of them, there came a gleam of grey twilight. It was Lightning who first spotted it, however, for his interest in the skull had quickly passed.

'Look!' he cried, pointing ahead, 'isn't that daylight?'

The answer lurked round the corner. They reached the bend and there at the top of a sharp rise in the tunnel lay a bright green medallion of light. It shifted about, and the boys saw that it was a way out to the open air and that it was guarded by a mass of foliage from a bush or tree blowing to and fro in a high wind.

As they climbed that last stage, the daylight strengthened so rapidly that it almost blinded them. They halted and switched off the two remaining torches, which were restored to their owners' knapsacks. With eyes accustomed to the wonderful light of day, the boys stared at tufts of grass and hart's-tongue ferns and trails of wild geranium

Lightning leaned forward and jumped into the open

which grew for many yards into the tunnel. The sandy bed shone like gold dust, and a trickle of russet moisture came out of the rock and soaked into it, changing the gold to bronze. Another minute passed and the expedition reached the top.

Lightning leaned forward with his arms outstretched like a diver and plunged into the green bush, parted it, and jumped into the open. The others followed him, and the five boys stood in a circle looking at each other wonderingly. Nobody spoke, for five strange faces were being studied for signs of the past experiences of a day in the underworld.

Only fatigue and dirt registered there, or so at first it seemed. John, however, that observant fellow with the new pair of spectacles, noticed something different in the expression of two of the members of the Tomahawk Club. The shy, self-effacing George Reynolds had changed: so had the cocksure Alan Hobbs. John could not look at himself, but as he felt no different he presumed that he was in the majority with Meaty Sanders and Lightning Soames, who were totally unchanged except for the dirt on their clothes and persons and the clot of plaster on Lightning's forehead.

John looked at his watch. 'Six-fifteen,' he said, and nodded significantly to George who was staring downhill in a meditative way.

'That gives us three-quarters of an hour,' he answered. 'Ample time, John.'

'Time for what?'

'To find where the river breaks through,' said George. 'We need to know that, don't we?'

John was too tired to answer, so he merely nodded assent, while breaking into a great yawn and stretching his cramped spine. Inwardly he was still excited by the events of the day and the discovery of the skull, but he was vaguely disappointed that the adventure had not been rounded off in a methodical way dear to his heart, by their emerging out of the opening where they had entered. He found himself wondering what animal it was which had directed him to that door, and he was a boy who hated to leave questions unanswered. He looked around him now and saw that once again the sun was sinking ahead of them where the hills ran down to the sea with the river curving round them. A smart wind was blowing inland, but the sky was a cloudless blue and golden sunshine soaked into everything, setting the hillside ablaze with a soft but penetrating light that made every bush a burning bush, and every flower a cup of coloured fire. The smell was good, too, rising from the warm heather that carpeted the hillside.

No doubt it was weariness that made them stand there in this poetic mood. Nobody wanted to move except Lightning.

'What are you all waiting for?' he cried impatiently. The only person who found an answer was Alan. Since emerging from the tunnel he had shrunk into himself, and now he stepped aside, turning his back on the others.

'I'm not going home,' he said.

'What do you mean?' said George sharply.

The reply came with greater obstinacy.

'I can't go home without the lamp. It might have been different if I'd asked for it, but even then he'd have flown into a rage. But as it is, he'll go raving mad, and my mother will get drawn into it, too. I tell you, you don't know what he's like. I tell you – !'

He choked, and once again he stumbled on to his knees and knelt there rocking himself to and fro in a paroxysm of terror.

The gentle evening sunshine fell on the bowed figure, and the faces of the four boys who stood there in misery looking at him. Meaty Sanders uttered a little moan of dismay and clasped himself nervously round the stomach. Little Soames changed from one leg to the other like a bird refusing to be caught. It was left to the other two to decide what was to be done. They appeared to think together, and to think alike, for simultaneously, they stepped forward, George taking Alan under one arm, John taking him under the other. Without a word their touch persuaded him to rise to his feet, and so the three of them began to walk down the hill, followed by Lightning and Meaty.

'Look, Alan!' said George, at last. 'Here's the spot where the river comes out. We were only a few feet from this an hour ago.'

There was no reply.

'The siphon looks dark from this side,' said John. He stooped down and peered into the mass of rushes and weeds growing round the exit from the rock. All he could see was a deepening of the colour of the stream, like the receding funnels of vegetation where a spring wells up in the bed of a millpond.

'It wouldn't have been much fun struggling through all that stuff this side of the siphon,' said George.

This remark apparently reminded Alan that it was he who had put the veto on the proposal to plunge through the siphon. The pleasure of being in the right restored him somewhat. He stopped struggling with himself, looked from one to the other of his companions, and then in a half-hearted way joined in the examination of the rock-face out of which the river poured rapidly, and as rapidly slowed down and spread out.

'You see, everything goes home in the end,' said John, with an old-fashioned tone in his voice. He spoke thoughtfully, staring at the stream, and he did not see George look at him with a gleam of amusement in his eyes.

'Yes, we'd all better get home,' he said. 'I'll come with you, if you like,' he added, turning to Alan.

By this time, however, Meaty was standing near by and he interrupted. 'No, I'm going home with him. It was my fault the lamp was lost. I kicked it out of his hand, so I can explain to his father. That ought to help a bit.'

This seemed to be conclusive, and it had the effect of encouraging Alan to do nothing foolhardy. From that time onward until they reached the outskirts of the town, a weary band, he and Meaty walked together at the head of the procession. The moment came for the party to break up, and it was Lightning who drifted away first like a butterfly passing from one blossom to the next, as light as a feather.

'Good-bye, all,' he cried, and fluttered away towards his home.

'Lightning Soames!' said George, looking after the wind-borne little figure as it flew up the road. There was a touch of sardonic envy in his heavy voice. Then he turned to John, saying, 'Well, we'd better get on. You two go the other way, don't you? Everything all right, Alan?'

Alan stared at him as though at a stranger, then suddenly recognized him, nodded, and turned nervously away. Meaty made a grimace which might mean anything, and lumbered off after him.

The two remaining boys stood and watched them for some minutes. Meaty towered above his companion, for Alan was still walking with a stoop as though cringing in anticipation of a blow. It was a sad moment, for not even a deserved retribution is an altogether cheering prospect.

And also the end of shared adventures leaves a sense of emptiness behind.

The sun was dropping behind the trees and two bats began to flit up and down the lane as though carrying messages to the two friends who could still not tear themselves away from the long last moment of the day's brotherhood.

'Well,' said George, 'time's running out, John. What is it now?'

John looked at his watch and in the falling light, the luminous hands and figures began to shine green. He did not know why, but this made him feel miserable as he replied:

'It wants twenty minutes to seven, and we've ten minutes walk from here.'

They set off towards home without another word, and continued in silence, the bats following them up and creaking past their heads like animated leather gloves. The minutes trickled past, and soon the boys found themselves at the gates of the drive of Dr Walters's house. Here they halted and looked at each other shyly. Before they could say good night, the Doctor drove up in his car. Seeing the boys, he stopped and poked his head out of the driver's window.

'Well, you've made it,' he said, 'but only just.' Then he

noticed the dirty handkerchief, and the odd way in which George was holding the dark-lantern in his bandaged hand.

'What have you done there, Reynolds?' The boy looked sheepish.

'Oh, nothing,' he said, 'just a slight burn, that's all.'

'Oh; did you not use the first-aid box?'

'No,' said George, 'I meant to, but we were in a spot of bother at that time and I was in a hurry.'

The doctor looked severe.

'I see. Who was in charge at that moment? You, John?'

'No, sir,' George answered. 'I was really looking after things then.'

'That makes it all the worse. If you were in charge you had no right to neglect yourself because you had the double responsibility, one to the party and one to yourself. That's a point to remember in future. A leader who starts being heroic in that kind of way is a dangerous man. Come up to the surgery and I will have a look at that hand. Burns can be unpleasant.'

A chastened George and an angry nephew followed the car up to the front door of the house. John was puzzled by his uncle's attitude to George, and he determined to tell the doctor what sort of a job his friend had made of the day's adventure. But George appeared to understand the doctor better and he bore no resentment; indeed, he was almost dog-like in his devotion and stood in the surgery following the doctor's movements with grateful eyes while his hand was being dressed.

'You see, it's not too clean, Reynolds. You've taken a risk there, my boy; a risk you could have avoided. That's where leadership comes in.' Then he grinned and put his arm round George's shoulders. 'That'll do,' he said. 'I'll dress it again tomorrow. Cut off home, now.' He lifted his blotting pad, took up a sealed envelope and handed it to his nephew. 'You'll want this John. I was coming back to open it.'

The boys left the surgery together and walked down the drive in the dusk. They reached the gate before either spoke.

'I wish I knew what it was that I saw running through the bracken on Sunday night,' said John. 'I hate leaving things unfinished.' His spectacles flashed in the half light so that George could not see his eyes. But the sagacious friend could read his thoughts.

'We'll find out about that. There's time before us. And there's that other tunnel to explore, too, when next we go to show the way to the skull.'

'I must plan that with my uncle tonight,' said John.

George moved away, saying, 'You've done enough for one day, John.' He walked a little farther, then stopped, fumbled in his pocket and came back.

He held out something in his hand.

'I forgot this.'

'What is it?'

'I found it in that little tunnel just as we started, and I remembered you said you'd lost it.'

It was the button off John's coat.

THE AUTHOR

RICHARD CHURCH was born in Battersea in 1893, and afterwards lived in Dulwich village. The first volume of his autobiography, *Over the Bridge,* describes his life in detail until he entered the Civil Service at the age of seventeen.

He followed his literary interests while he was in the Civil Service, which he left in 1935 to become literary adviser to Dent the publishers until 1952, when he took the same position with Hutchinson for a year.

Richard Church lives in a converted oasthouse in Kent, which is very spacious and simple. He works in a sound-proofed room on a hill-top, with a wide view across a wooded valley.

He is well known as a poet and essayist, and is also a successful novelist. The third volume of his autobiography was published in 1964. Besides writing itself, he takes an active part in literary affairs, and is a prominent member of the P.E.N. Club and on the selection board of the Book Society. He says he is as much interested in good speech and music as literature, and believes that good writing will make good hearing.